The Story and Promise of Vatican II
in Plain English

Also by Bill Huebsch

Group Reading Guide for The Joy of the Gospel
(Twenty-Third Publications, 2013)

The Spiritual Wisdom of St. John XXIII
(Twenty-Third Publications, 2014)

Jesus: The Master Catechist
(Twenty-Third Publications, 2015)

Group Reading Guide for the Care of our Common Home
(Twenty-Third Publications, 2015)

Be Merciful: The Spiritual and Corporal Works of Mercy
(Twenty-Third Publications, 2015)

Group Reading Guide for The Joy of Love
(Twenty-Third Publications, 2016)

Our Catholic Life | Nuestra Vida Católica
(Twenty-Third Publications, 2016)

How to Live Well & Do Good
(Amazon.com, 2016)

How to Recognize Grace When You See It
(Amazon.com, 2016)

The Art of Accompaniment
(Twenty-Third Publications, 2017)

How God Speaks to Us in Prayer
(Amazon.com, 2017)

Group Reading Guide for Rejoice & Be Glad
(Twenty-Third Publications, 2018)

Promise and Hope: Pastoral Theology in the Age of Mercy
(Twenty-Third Publications, 2020)

The Story and Promise of Vatican II
in Plain English

Revised and Updated

Bill Huebsch

✷ The Pastoral Center

Direct quotations from the documents of Vatican II are taken from the official Vatican website at http://www.Vatican.va.

This is the second edition of this work. It was previously published in 1997 under the title *Vatican II in Plain English* by Thomas More Books and later acquired by Ave Maria Press in the early 2000s. The first edition is now out of print.

Second edition, March 2020

Published by The Pastoral Center, 1212 Versailles Ave, Alameda, CA 94501. http://pastoral.center

ISBN 978-1-949628-24-1

Table of Contents

*Comprehensive summaries of the remaining twelve council
documents can be found at http://Vatican2.center.*

Introduction

History, as Pope John XXIII[1] once said, is the teacher of life. We cannot understand the present moment in which we live without understanding what has come before us. Pope John had been a teacher of history in the seminary in Bergamo, Italy, his home diocese, and he had a strong understanding of the history of the church. He had also lived in eastern Europe for a couple of decades—which gave him ecumenical and international experience. But it was while he served as papal nuncio to France after World War II that the idea of a council may have begun to gel for him. It was there—in France—where he met many of those who would later play a significant role in Vatican II. Paris then was a swirl of new approaches to theology, liturgy, history, ecumenism, and our understanding of the church. Likewise, nearby Belgium, Germany, Austria, and the Netherlands had busy academic circles. Around the world, more and more bishops were well-trained theologians. Without anyone being consciously aware of it, the Holy Spirit in those days was preparing the church—and Angelo Roncalli—for the Second Vatican Council.

Many popes in the history of the church have been chosen from the leading families of Rome or Italy, but Roncalli came from humble, rural beginnings in the northern Italian village of Sotto il Monte. They were farmers, a close-knit and hard-working family. He remained tightly connected to this family throughout his life, and, at the time of his death, they were standing at his bedside.

It was said that, when asked about why a council was needed, Pope John responded with a historical reference. "It's time," he's reported to have said, "to sweep the imperial dust off the throne of St. Peter, which has gathered there since Constantine." Indeed, much of what the council did was to restore elements of the early church—the first three hundred or so years—and update them for the modern times. When Constantine brought the church into his political center and lavished privilege on its clergy in the early 300s, many elements that made the church vibrant and alive were lost.

The catechumenate, an early pathway into the faith, had been closed down since the Constantinian period. The diaconate, an

1

office in the early church organized to serve the poor, had like-wise been lost. The participation by all the baptized in the Mass had been replaced with a clergy-centered liturgy while laypeople became spectators. Baptism itself, once the essential sacerdotal sacrament—that is, the sacrament which commissioned everyone as a pastoral minister—had become a sort of magical way to erase original sin. Baptisms were "performed" after Mass in the back of our churches while ordination had become the largest liturgical celebration of the diocese each year with fanfare and pomp galore. Baptism was thus an afterthought, and ordination was always in the foreground. Faith as a personal relationship with Jesus had been replaced with mere assent to a set of doctrinal propositions. The life of discipleship and the desire to follow the teachings of Jesus had been replaced with "minimum obligations" imposed under pain of mortal sin. The church itself, once a sign to the world of Jesus who is the Christ, a sacrament of his risen presence, of his love and mercy, had become an institution often mired in politics, armies, inquisitions, and rigidity. And on and on. Indeed, "the imperial dust of Constantine."

Then along came this council, throwing open the windows of the church, inviting everyone to a renewed encounter with Jesus, opening itself to the world, welcoming guests from outside our walls, and seeking its way as a pilgrim. The church was restored in Jesus, who is the Christ. The story and promise of Vatican II point the way forward for us. They are the bedrock on which the current renewal of pastoral theology is firmly set.

Many of the characteristics of Vatican II set it apart from previous councils:

- The presence of non-Roman Catholic observers, including representatives of the Russian Church for the first time in hundreds of years, was a landmark. Present were representatives from Protestant, Anglican, Orthodox, and Jewish churches.
- The sheer number of participants was staggering compared to past councils. Vatican I had 800 participants, Vatican II, nearly 2,500.
- The genuinely international flavor was also new for the church. Most bishops at Vatican I and all previous councils had been European, even those attending from other continents, but this was indeed a worldwide body of prelates.

- The presence of a press corps—even though not always well informed by the *official* press office—suggested a new openness and an awareness that the world was watching and listening.
- With all these people present, Vatican II was the largest such gathering in the history of the church.
- Vatican II was the first ecumenical council to have electricity, telephones, cars, airplanes, typewriters, and computerized voting.
- For the first time in history, a council of the whole church was meeting without the interference of any temporal government. It was the first since the eighth century to meet at a time when there was complete separation of church and state in Italy and south-central Europe. This gave the council a more pastoral tone. It removed past political tendencies and pointed to true renewal.
- And finally, this council's focus on animating the faith of Christians rather than defining doctrine or condemning heretics was also new.

Why this book?

Of course, much has already been written about the Second Vatican Council. The original documents are readily available in many languages today, online and in print. Numerous scholarly books in the market deal with the history and theology of the council. There is so much excellent material, in fact, that wading through it can be daunting for the average reader. Many people know the importance of understanding this remarkable religious event. They often pick up the council's final documents or its theology to get started but, after reading a few articles of one or the other, they put them back down again. Both the history and the documents can make for dense reading.

This volume takes its place among the Vatican II books in a unique space. It provides a brief telling of the story of the council in plain English, following an exciting chronological pathway from the beginning of the council to its final bell. Knowing the story is vital to understanding the documents and the newly established pastoral tone which Vatican II gave to the church. At the end of the chronology, each of the documents is summarized for the reader.

Following this opening section is a presentation in plain English of the four constitutions from the council. These constitutions remain the normative guiding documents for today's church. They were a significant source for the *Catechism,* cited more often there than any document other than Sacred Scripture. They have not been changed, reduced, or set aside in any way since the council ended in 1965. There are also a dozen other decrees and declarations from Vatican II, and these are also available to the reader online as full article-by-article paraphrases. Hence all sixteen council documents in plain English are an essential part of this project.

Sources

The first credit in my research must go to a professor of history at the Catholic Theological Union of Chicago in 1980, Fr Ted Ross SJ. His courses on the Second Vatican Council provided treatments of all the primary sources that were then available on the council. His excellent lectures, faith, wit, and deep understanding of the council inspired me to adopt Vatican II as an area of great interest in my graduate studies and in the ministry work that followed for the next forty years.

Another primary source of inspiration and information for me was the late Bishop Ray Lucker of the Diocese of New Ulm in Minnesota. Ray was in Rome during the Second Vatican Council and was deeply moved and changed by it. Immediately after graduate school, I worked on the pastoral team in the New Ulm Diocese alongside him and other remarkable people and got a "second education" from that experience. The original idea for this project came from Ray Lucker. Here in part is how Ray felt about his time in Rome:

> Twelve years after I was ordained, I was sent to Rome to study theology. I was there during the Second Vatican Council. It was the most profound experience of my life. I went through personal conversion. My faith became a personal relationship with God as well as an assent to the truths that God has revealed. The Council called the whole church to reform and renewal, for an active, informed and committed laity… and invited every member of the church to work for the transformation of society…. I saw in the Second Vatican Council a fulfillment of all of my dreams.[2]

I first went to work on this twenty-five years ago in the mid-1990s, working with Paul Thurmes, a brilliant scholar who is fluent in Italian. The first translation from Latin for most Roman documents was usually to Italian. In this revised edition, as in the original, I also consulted the primary sources considered trustworthy by everyone, including the final published documents from the council, both the English translations[3] as well as the original Latin[4]. I pored over and outlined the council based on the "Daybooks" of the council published in English.[5] The Daybooks are essentially the "minutes" of Vatican II and are filled with details on the speeches, voting, and related events that formed the council. They're a rich source for understanding how the council unfolded in real time. I found and studied the reflections of the council's participants, both the bishops and the theological experts who were present[6]. And I have read and re-read the history of this council[7].

I also studied the accounts given by Xavier Rynne[8], published first as a series of columns in *The New Yorker* and still an absolutely excellent telling of the story, and Bob Kaiser's excellent coverage[9], which appeared first in *Time* magazine, as well as many other commentaries, news articles, and theological texts.

I have also been participating in the liturgy of the church restored by the council. This is that place where—week after week—we experience firsthand the life we share together about which the council was so concerned.

More recently, I have been teaching courses on the council and the resulting pastoral theology in the Institute for Pastoral Studies at the Loyola University of Chicago. Likewise, I have been lecturing to groups in the U.S., Canada, and England on this remarkable event, the most important religious event of the last century. Lately, my teaching texts have been two secondary sources: *What Happened at Vatican II?* by Jesuit John W. O'Malley[10] along with *Keys to the Council* by Richard Gaillardetz and Catherine Clifford[11]. Both of these texts are absolutely top-notch. I also ask my students to read the documents in this plain English version as a way to help them understand the actual texts themselves.

Because I have been immersed in so many primary sources—and I have hundreds of pages of my own notes, reflections, observations, and insights—much of that from my original research more than twenty-five years ago, a lot of it handwritten or typed, some of it from Paul Thurmes, Ted Ross or Ray Lucker—I cite specific sources in this revision only when I actually quote other scholars or lift an idea directly from them. This text was substantially written in the 1990s and is being updated here only where new research has provided further information or insights. My original version is still remarkably accurate. The endnotes also form the bibliography. My thanks go to the very competent staff of the John Ireland Library at the University of St. Thomas, St. Paul, MN, for their help in this project.

My Purposes

Again, the goal of this project, building on all the work that has been done by others, is to (1) provide in plain English a brief explanation of the story of the council by following its events in chronological order, and (2) to help the reader see the promise of the council in the texts of the documents themselves. The story is told in standard paragraph form set within a chronology. The documents are presented here as a poetic paraphrased summary using sense lines instead of sentences (as they were in the 1996 edition), inviting the reader to go to the original text to have a first-hand, primary source. I have retained the article numbers from those original texts to help students and readers find their way. The poetic sense lines allow for the juxtaposition of ideas and the isolation of critical thoughts and phrases. They're meant to inspire and edify the reader at the level of the heart and soul, as well as the mind and intellect.

How we read church documents

Church documents have authority based on both (1) where they fall in "the hierarchy of papal pronouncements" as well as (2) how they are "received" by the faithful. There are, in total, some fifty different types of papal or Roman documents. Among them, decretal letters and constitutions rank very high, especially constitutions from an ecumenical council. A decretal letter may be used to declare an infallible doctrine or to pronounce the canonization of a saint. A constitution may be used to declare a teaching which is of a substantial nature, one that is central to the entire church. No decretal letters but four important constitutions were promulgated at Vatican II addressing (1) the church as such (or *ad intra*), (2) the liturgy, (3) divine revelation, and (4) the church's relationship to the modern world (or *ad extra*).

Also at a high rank are papal bulls, *motu proprios,* and encyclicals. A papal bull, named after its red seal, or *bulla* in Italian, is a very solemn pronouncement. One was issued to convoke Vatican II, for example. A *motu proprio* is a more personal papal decree, written by the pope himself, signed in his own hand. One was used to declare the rules and procedures for the council, for example. An encyclical is somewhat lower in rank, used to declare the social and moral teachings of the church. There were no encyclicals issued as official documents of Vatican II.

Significantly lower in rank are addresses or allocutions and papal speeches used to give the opinion of the pope or to make an announcement. At about that same rank are decrees and declarations, of which there were a total of twelve at Vatican II. A decree gives a significant teaching but one that requires further discussion while a declaration usually addresses an area that may be, by its nature, controversial or in need of further doctrinal development. Close in rank to these are instructions that are used to amplify other documents and give specific steps to carry them out. Below these at various levels of rank are documents giving the opinions of the Roman Curia and other prelates.

Documents published by a council are considered very authoritative because they're prepared by such a broad consultation among bishops and the pope and because they reflect the thinking of the church. But another factor in measuring their relative authority is how the men and women of the church *receive* them and understand them. This "doctrine of reception" is how the church has always allowed for the Holy Spirit to speak through all the baptized. "The canonical doctrine of reception, broadly stated, asserts that for a law or rule to be an effective guide for the believing community, it must be accepted by that community."[12]

A Chronological & Annotated Outline of the Major Events of the Second Vatican Council

The Period Before the Council
October 1959 to September 1962

October 9, 1958 ▶ **Pope Pius XII** died.

October 28, 1958 ▶ **Angelo Roncalli** was elected pope and took the name of John XXIII.

January 25, 1959 ▶ **Pope John XXIII announced his intention to call the council.** He announced three initiatives: (1) his plan to convene the council, (2) his decision to hold a synod in the Diocese of Rome, and (3) his plan to revise the code of canon law. His announcement was met with little support from the leaders of the Roman Curia.

Background

Why, after 400 years of living out the decrees and rubrics of the Council of Trent and the post-Tridentine church, did Vatican II occur? How did the modern church succeed in initiating such sweeping reforms? Why now? Why these particular reforms? **How did all this start?**

On the one hand, the answer is plain: nothing less than the entire history of the church set the stage on which this council unfolded. All the previous twenty worldwide councils. All the other regional and local councils and synods over the centuries—literally, hundreds of them. All the theologians, reformers, popes, and leaders throughout the ages. All the saints. All the scandals and corruption. All the faithful people, hungering for the deposit of Christian faith. All of it—the people and events of the church's history—formed the backdrop of this council. Nothing less.

History is like that. It unfolds at its own speed like a great, centuries-long conversation, offering people in every age the opportunity to contribute in their own day. Lucky the ones who speak up when their turn arrives for they become the force that molds the world.

On the other hand, the answer might also have been simply that some minor event within the Vatican itself moved Pope John

XXIII to decide for reform. Perhaps some petty rule was broken, which resulted in a quarrel among the members of the curia. Or maybe some rubric was not followed, causing a scrupulous rubricist to ask the pope's forgiveness. Pope John may have said to himself at any such moment that *some*thing had to be done about such pettiness, *some*one had to clean out the closets of a Vatican too long without reform.

Nonetheless, the extraordinary announcement that a worldwide council of the Roman Catholic Church would be held was a surprise to everyone, including, it seems, Pope John himself. But the origin of the idea in Pope John's own mind is not complicated. He was simply struck by a strong intuition that the time for such a council was now. He became convinced in a moment of certainty that the Holy Spirit was about to hover over the church, stirring it up, rising like daybreak, forerunning a most splendid light.

He told this story in his opening speech at the council. Speaking of the origin of the idea itself, he said he wished to record for history his own personal account "of the first sudden bringing up in our heart and lips of the simple words, 'ecumenical council.'... It was completely unexpected," he said, "like a flash of heavenly light, shedding sweetness in eyes and hearts. And at the same time, it gave rise to a great fervor throughout the world in expectation of the holding of the council."

His decision to go forward with this impulse, interestingly, did not result from a "Vatican self-study" performed by consultants and processed through endless committees, lugging ring-bound photocopies of plans, budgets, and opinion polls around the Vatican.

Instead, it resulted from his personal attention to that "flash of heavenly light," which arose in his soul and breast. It resulted from his trust in the Holy Spirit. And he did not hesitate. He had been pope only a couple of months when this happened, scarcely time to find one's way through the labyrinthine corridors of the Vatican. Then, speaking to 17 cardinals at the Basilica of St. Paul-Outside-the-Walls in Rome on this date, the feast of St. Paul, January 25, 1959, he announced his intention to hold Vatican II.

Ecumenical. It should be noted that the term *ecumenical council,* as it is used in reference to Vatican II, does not mean that it would be an "interfaith council." The term *ecumenical* used in this context simply means "worldwide." When used in most other settings in today's church, it means interreligious, especially between Protestants and Catholics, Anglicans and Catholics, or Eastern Orthodox and Catholics. But even though this would not be an interfaith council of Christians as such, Pope John did make clear his intention to invite all of these "separated brethren" to be present as guests.

Let's take a look at his remarks, presented here in summary form as a paraphrase in sense lines.

Pope John XXIII's Announcement of Vatican II
Made at the Basilica of St. Paul-Outside-the-Walls
January 25, 1959

I am prompted to open my mind and heart to you,
    here on this feast of the Conversion of St. Paul.
I want to tell you frankly about several points
    of planned pastoral activity
    which have emerged in my thoughts
        during my brief three months here
        within these church circles in Rome.
In doing so, I am thinking of the care of the souls
    of the faithful in these modern times.

I know that everyone is watching me
    as the new pope,
    wondering what kind of time this will be
        for the church.
I am gradually settling into my new role
    and beginning to see how it will fit
    into the overall history of the church.
As you know, I have a double responsibility
    as both bishop of the Diocese of Rome
    and Shepherd of the universal church.
I am paying attention to both of these as I should.

First, let me reflect on the City of Rome.
It is much changed since my own youth
    and is now a bustling city with rapid growth,
        especially in the suburbs,

struggling at times to be a united community.
I have been briefed on the spiritual condition
     of the people in Rome
     and I am pleased with the wonderful efforts
          of the cardinal vicar,
          who handles the day-to-day activities
               of this local diocese.
He and his staff have been vigilant and zealous
     in providing for the local needs.

But, on the other hand,
          I remember the story in the Gospels
          when the great crowds called on Jesus
          to help them find nourishment and grace.
It touches my heart as I think of it:
          a few loaves, a few fish,
          "what are these among so many?!"
This says it all: an increase in energies
          and a more coordinated effort will, with God's help,
               produce great fruits!
I fervently desire this more fruitful
          and profoundly spiritual life for the church.

It is a happy thing to see the grace of Jesus
          multiplied throughout the world
          and providing guidance and blessing for everyone.
But I am saddened when people forget
          the place of God in their lives
          and pursue earthly goods,
          as though they were an end in themselves.
I think, in fact, that this blind pursuit
          of the things of this world
          emerges from the power of darkness,
               not from the light of the Gospels,
               and it is enabled by technology.
All of this weakens the energy of the Spirit
          and generally, leads to divisions,
               spiritual decline,
               and moral failure.

As a priest, and now as the shepherd of the church,
　　　　I am troubled and aroused
　　　　by this tendency in modern life
　　　　　　　and this makes me determined
　　　　　　　to recall certain ancient practices of the church
　　　　　　　　　in order to remedy this.
Throughout the history of the church,
　　　　such renewal has always yielded results.
It produces greater clarity of thought,
　　　　the solidarity of religious unity,
　　　　and abundant spiritual riches in people's lives.

So now, trembling a bit with emotion,
　　　　I announce to you my intention
　　　　to hold a twofold event:
　　　　　　　a diocesan-wide meeting for this city
　　　　　　　and an ecumenical council
　　　　　　　　　for the universal church.
And this will also lead to a bringing up-to-date
　　　　of the code of canon law,
　　　　which will accompany and crown
　　　　　　　these other two events.
For the moment, my announcement to you
　　　　is sufficiently made,
　　　　and I will also announce this myself
　　　　to the rest of the cardinals of the world.
I would be happy to hear your opinion of this
　　　　and also grateful for your suggestions
　　　　as to how to best carry out this triple plan.
In moving forward like this,
　　　　I am trusting in God's grace,
　　　　as well as the protection and intercession
　　　　　　　of Mary and the saints.

I beg them for blessings on this work:
　　　　a good beginning,
　　　　a blessed continuation,
　　　　and a happy outcome.
We think this will produce a great enlightenment
　　　　for all Christian people

as well as a renewed invitation
> to our separated sisters and brothers
> so that all may follow us
> in this search for unity and grace.

In closing, let me recite the blessing
> of St. Leo the Great,
> which is so fitting for this moment in time:
"You are my crown and my joy if your faith,
> which, from the beginning of the Gospels,
> > is preached throughout the world,
> > perseveres in sweetness and holiness."
Oh! What a greeting this is,
> wholly worthy of our spiritual family.
I bless you in the name of the Father
> and of the Son
> and of the Holy Spirit. Amen.

After he concluded this short allocution to the cardinals at St. Paul's, he paused and waited. Silence followed. No one spoke. Not one of the cardinals expressed a single thought. Pope John wrote about this in his journal later. "Humanly, I could have expected that the cardinals, after hearing my announcement, might have crowded around to express approval and good wishes…Instead, there was a devout and impressive silence."[13] Pope John never lost his sense of humor.

Not only were the cardinals silent that day in St. Paul's, but many of them were alarmed. Here was this new pope, an old man when he was elected, announcing an ecumenical council, the first since 1870. Was he out of his mind? They may have wondered. Did he know what he was saying? But John was indeed in his right mind, and he knew exactly what he was saying. He proved this to them one by one as time went on and the preparations for Vatican II got underway in earnest.

January 24–31, 1960 ▶ **The synod in the Diocese of Rome,** which he announced in the speech you just read was indeed held. Called by the pope, this synod was intended to renew the faith of the people of Rome.

Background

It should be noted that a synod is an official meeting of the church at pretty much any level: international, national, regional, or diocesan. Synods usually have quite specific, limited goals and produce statements and pastoral letters aimed at guiding the church in its everyday life.

To keep this synod focused on his own desired outcomes, Pope John decided to do the speaking at the Roman synod himself. In the end, he gave several talks which treated a rather wide range of faith issues, including:

- Belief in God as a trinity of love.
- Redemption from sin by the earthly sufferings and death of Jesus, the Christ.
- The Resurrection and the hope of seeing God face to face.
- The pitfalls and dangers of modern life that may lead to damnation.

For the fourth issue, Pope John insisted on the *via positiva*: modern women and men, by putting their shoulder to the wheel of life, he argued, can achieve decency, stability, security, and a touch of holiness, no matter what the living conditions in which they find themselves. Article 35 of the synodal statues also provides for more compassionate treatment of priests who have left the church or the priesthood than was prevalent in the recent past.

Canons. Many of the notions he articulated at this synod were later reflected in the opening sections of the Constitution on the Church. It should be noted, however, that nearly every public statement which emerged from this week-long Synod were canons—and there were 755 of these canons! A canon is a short, prescriptive rule or norm that includes a penalty for failure to obey. A canon often begins with the language, "If anyone does not believe in such and such…" and ends with the phrase, "… then *anathema sit!*" St. Paul used the term *anathema* in Galatians 1:8. Later it referred to a form of ex-communication under church law. It means 'If someone doesn't agree with this doctrine or dogma and follow it to the letter, then let him or her be reviled, shunned, or even damned.' See what I mean? A bit negative. This penalty of ex-communication, by the way, was eliminated with the promulgation of the 1983 revised Code.

Such canons had been in use in the church since the early 300s. The canons in the Roman synod in 1960—all of which had been prepared before the synod convened—dealt with regulatory minutiae, and they were in this negative tone which had prevailed in church announcements for centuries. Observers hoping for church reform at the council did not find in this synod a robust model of the *via positiva*, despite John's hopes and example. It should be noted, however, that not a single canon was issued from Vatican II.

May 17, 1959 ▶ Pope John took a significant first step toward organizing the council by establishing an **Ante-preparatory Commission**. He named Cardinal Tardini as its head.

Throughout the preparatory period, he faced stiff opposition from members of his own curia and others who feared doom for the church if the event were actually to occur. These church insiders, about whom he spoke in his opening speech, had come to believe that only they were able to guide and direct the church. They feared that bringing 2,500 bishops and cardinals to Rome from all over the world, many of them already asking challenging questions, would lead only to disaster. But Pope John's resolve to proceed overrode all their concerns. It was said[14] that each time a Vatican official approached Pope John with a suggestion for postponement of Vatican II, he advanced the target starting date by one month!

If this is true, it was propitious because his original plan had been to convene the council in the fall of 1963. It actually began on October 11, 1962, preceding his death by only eight months.

June 18, 1959 ▶ **The formal preparation for Vatican II began** with a worldwide consultation with some 2,500 residential bishops, heads of male religious orders, and male faculty members of Catholic universities. It was Pope John's desire to know what the leaders of the church around the world were thinking. What were the most pressing issues of faith?

Background

The consultation got underway through an invitation sent by Cardinal Tardini, Pope John's secretary of state. The message asked the bishops of the world to express their desires for the council.

Tardini's letter encouraged the bishops to offer their ideas "with complete freedom and honesty...on anything Your Excellency thinks should be treated in the council"[15].

The pope sought advice and suggestions from 2,594 members of the world's hierarchy in 134 nations. More than 75 percent participated. It should be noted that this entire consultation occurred before the advent of the modern means of communication we have today. It produced more than five thousand pages of material, all manually typed or written. Their letters were photocopied and filed. Their ideas were then grouped by category and subject. All of this took place on the third floor of one of the newer office buildings near the entrance to the piazza of St. Peter's. The work was headed by Archbishop Pericle Felici, who was considered strict but conservative and who had been chosen to serve as secretary of the Ante-Preparatory phase.

Archbishop Felici was later named secretary-general of the council itself and proved to be an excellent one because he was a skilled Latinist and quick-witted presider. Although he favored the cause of the more cautious bishops who feared reform, he kept the meetings in order by frequent admonitions and humorous interjections, which allowed for free conciliar debate.

The work of organizing all this input was detailed and painstaking—and took the better part of six months to accomplish. Most of the responses were submitted in Latin, and the effort to study them, determine their subject area, and file them appropriately was made by only five priests working with Archbishop Felici. Once work on the bishops' responses was completed, the group began work on the responses received from the theological universities of the world, along with those received from the various offices of the curia itself.

All of this material was eventually collated and printed in book form. The books were then passed along to a group of preparatory commissions that were instituted by Pope John at a solemn Vespers on Pentecost Sunday, June 5, 1960.

Mid-1960 ▶ **Close Vatican I.** A needed and technical step before Vatican II would convene was to declare Vatican I officially closed. It had been adjourned because of the Franco-Prussian War in 1870 and the siege of Rome by Italian nationalists, but it had never been formally closed. The formal closing of Vatican I was a clear sign to the world and to the leaders of the church that Vatican II would not be a mere *continuation* of the First Vatican Council, but a new and free-standing council with its own agenda.

June 5, 1960 ▶ Pope John issued a *motu proprio* announcing that the Ante-preparatory work was completed and that the time had come **"to proceed, with God's help, to the setting up of the commissions"** which would **"devote themselves to the study of the matters"** that would be **"discussed at the council."** These commissions, he went on to say, would be composed of cardinals, bishops, and other church workers noted for their virtue and learning, from both the diocesan and religious clergy, chosen from different parts of the world, so that, in this respect also, the catholicity of the church might be displayed.

Background

A *motu proprio* is a papal statement that is prepared and signed by the pope himself and which states his personal wishes about a matter. In the hierarchy of papal pronouncements, *motu proprios* rank quite high. Pope John kept his own hand in the entire process of preparing for this council.

On this same day ▶ Pope John also outlined what he wanted **the operating procedure for this council to be**. It would begin, he said, with an introductory and exploratory phase, which was just concluded. It would then proceed into a preparatory stage that was started that day. The preparatory period would be under the guidance of the commissions that he established. It would be coordinated by a central coordinating commission which would prepare position papers called *schemas* for the bishops of the world to consider in the general daily congregations of the council itself. The final phase of council proceedings, Pope John said in this address, would be the promulgation of the outcomes.

In this same address, he drew a distinction between the running of day-to-day church matters by the curia and the work of this council. The pope explained that "the preparation of the council would not be the task of the Roman Curia but, together with the illustrious prelates and consultors of the Roman Curia, bishops and scholars from all over the world will offer their contributions.

This distinction is therefore precise: the ordinary government of the church with which the Roman curia is concerned is one matter and the council another."

Behind the scenes, the officials of the curia viewed all this rapid preparation with attitudes ranging from passive agreement and light cooperation to outright alarm. They seemed not to trust the pope, not to believe he understood the church and the world as they did. They seemed to think that only they could adequately settle questions of the modern church. Realizing that they were not loved throughout the world, the officials of the curia seemed to fear that assembling all the bishops of the church in Rome would strip them of their power.

They also feared the liturgical movement, which was active in northern Europe, Canada, and the Midwestern United States. They were already flooded with demands for the use of the vernacular language—shocking!—something Luther had wanted! They also considered the new approach to biblical study dangerous, even though it was based on Pius XII's own encyclical *Divino Afflante Spiritu.*

Nouvelle Théologie. These fearful Vatican insiders saw the new theological movement—the *Nouvelle Théologie* as it was known in French—as a threat from the North, just as their predecessors had seen the Reformation of the sixteenth century. These modern reformers seemed to want many of the same things that were at the heart of the "troubles" of the 16th century: vernacular language in the Mass and other sacraments, biblical study by laypeople, the reform of the clergy and episcopacy, and a restructuring of the curia with a more collegial approach to authority. "Here they come again!" they must have thought.

Ressourcement. One feature of this new theology was to "return to the sources" of the church, to Scripture and the Fathers, to the apostolic years before Constantine and all that followed from that period. This return to the sources—known as *ressourcement* in French—rooted theology in the church's origins, which were far earlier than the Council of Trent. This was seen as a threat to those fearful of reform. Combined with Pope John's idea for *aggiornamento*—which means bringing the church up to date—the members of the curia saw a formula for disaster in the church: *Nouvelle Théologie, ressourcement, and aggiornamento.* The questions before the church would be addressed in the council through the application of these methods. Disaster!

And indeed, to some in the church even today, the work and results of Vatican II are still seen as that feared disaster.

In Rome, memories are long, and time passes slowly. To these members of the curia, it must have seemed as though all these questions had just been settled recently, even though *recently* would have meant 400 years earlier.

The pope, of course, was of a completely different mind. He wanted to bring the church up-to-date. He did not fear the biblical scholars and theologians; he looked to them to assist in preparing for his great renewal of church life. Reunion of the Christian churches, something feared and opposed in Vatican circles, was his life dream and his heart's fondest desire. Pope John addressed the fears of his closest circle of assistants and advisers in his opening address at the council, as we shall see here momentarily.

The insiders, however, shocked by the pope's obviously firm intentions, not to mention his resistance to their warnings, rallied to control the outcomes of the council as much as possible by gaining positions of power and influence in the preparatory commissions. **They appointed trusted "safe" men from various parts of the world to the leadership positions of these commissions and pointedly omitted inviting certain theologians or bishops they considered too "dangerous."** They couldn't control the Central Commission (which coordinated council activities and preparation and whose president was the pope himself), so they did the next best thing—they arranged to have the more cautious bishops who feared reform (Cardinals Ottaviani, Ruffini, Siri, Pizzardo, and Marella) lead the discussions.

Furthermore, they saw to it that published reports of the preparatory meetings reflected their aims and points of view. They took great pains to develop an interlocking system of control: bishops and monsignors, all Italian, named as members of the preparatory commissions. It should be noted that these men were acting out of faith. They held the most profound conviction that renewal would endanger the church somehow.

What was alarming for the rest of the church was that these men felt free to attack the church itself, but did not allow anyone else to do so or even to hint at such criticism. An example of this was an attack on the new biblical scholarship which was going on before the council and which helped give rise to a new understanding of divine revelation. Cardinal Ruffini of Palermo, himself a specialist in biblical research, rejected the new biblical studies and believed the Bible could be read only in fundamentalist, literalist terms. He published an article on page one of *L'Osservatore Romano* in June 1961 (before the first general meeting of the council) in which he directly contradicted Pius XII's encyclical on the matter, quoting the encyclical itself and calling the pope's position "absurd."

Anyone outside the curial circle would have been shipped off to exile for such a statement: his published works would have been recalled, and he would have been forced to recant. But this curial insider was praised by his curial colleagues for his objections and conservatism. Again, note that Ruffini and his colleagues were no doubt acting in good faith. They certainly must have believed that what they did was best for the church.

In contrast to these church insiders were many of the bishops of the world where the church was already undergoing rapid and massive change. Vatican II did not precipitate the modern times and modern thinking; it only gave it focus and theological reflection.

One example of this new ecclesial thinking and behavior was **Bishop Dammert Bellido of Cajamarca, Peru**, who declared, "One area in which, with the best of intentions, we still provoke scandal in some and disgust in others is in the lack of simplicity in the decoration of our churches and the riches with which we surround our ceremonies. In all innocence, we stretch our resources to obtain the costliest ornaments, which are in doubtful taste to begin with while, at the same time, the children of God are suffering from hunger, sickness, and misery. This is a true cause for scandal in the church today. Sumptuosity is not in accord with the poverty of our age." Indeed, the council embraced this point of view in the Constitution on the Liturgy, in chapter seven, where it said in #124 that in decorating churches, pastors should "strive after noble beauty rather than sumptuous display."

In many parts of the world, bishops were giving up their palaces and living among the poor. A group of bishops in Argentina became known as the "bishops with wooden crosses and crosiers." In San Antonio, Texas, Archbishop Lucey was a champion of social justice for the *braceros* or Mexican migrant workers. Even before the council, it was apparent to a world observer that it was no longer "business as usual" for the modern church.

Many other bishops in the world were well-trained theologians, reflecting on questions of faith and morals themselves, independently of the curia. Many of them became essential players at the council itself: Frings of Cologne, Lienart of Lille, Alfrink of Holland, Meyer of Chicago (the largest diocese in the world with 2.1 million Catholics at the time). Cardinal Montini is said to have taken 90 cases of books with him to Milan when he moved there from Rome to become its new archbishop (and later Pope Paul VI[16]).

Also among the scholarly bishops were Wright of Pittsburgh and Hallinan of Atlanta, known for their deep understanding of the modern times and their reflection on the church's place in them. Koenig of Vienna had written extensively on comparative religions. Bea and Suenens were theologians as well as cardinals and played significant roles in leading the movement for reform at the council.

Bishops all over the world were struggling long before Vatican II to find ways to make the church more compelling for the modern times. Experiments were going on in many parts of the world, from India, where Bishop Pereira had visited every village along the coast to introduce a program of modern social development, to Latin America, where bishops were taking up residence as pastors among the poor, to the Low Countries of Europe where Benedictines had their altars facing the people in the 1920s.

Meanwhile, the preparation by the commissions established by Pope John continued under the influence of all these forces, gradually coalescing in the months before the council to set the stage for the great debates which eventually occurred in the council hall.

December 25, 1961 ▶ **Pope John issued a *bull*** formally convoking the Second Vatican Council.

February 5, 1962 ▶ **Pope John set the opening date of the council** for October 11, 1962, the feast of the Divine Maternity of Mary. In so doing, he tied this council to the memory of the Council of Ephesus in 431, which defined the doctrine of Mary as the *Theot-okos*, which means "Mother of God."

July 20, 1962 ▶ Invitations were sent to **separated Christians (Protestant, Anglican, and Orthodox),** encouraging them to send observers to the council.

September 5, 1962 ▶ **The rules and procedures under which the council would operate were established** and published by another *motu proprio* issued only five weeks before the council opened. In this pronouncement, the pope

- named a presiding council
- named cardinals of the curia to head the ten council commissions responsible for the working documents or *schemas*
- appointed Cardinal Cicognani, the pope's secretary of state, as president of a particular office which would oversee unforeseen problems at the council
- required a two-thirds majority (in addition to his own approval) to enact decrees at the council itself, and regulated the rest of the voting
- invited non-Catholic observers to attend both the solemn public sessions and also the actual working sessions in which all the bishops would take part
- required bishops to remain in Rome throughout the council sessions and to leave only if they were given explicit permission to do so
- established that the meetings of the council would be held at the Vatican in St. Peter's
- directed what the bishops, abbots, and other prelates were to wear to the various council sessions: "At the public sessions all the fathers having episcopal rank…will wear a white cope and miter. But at the general congregations [daily meetings] the cardinals will wear red or violet cassocks, according to the liturgical season, with rochet, short cape, and mozzetta; patriarchs will dress in violet…abbots…will wear their own choir dress."
- established norms for a profession of faith and an oath of secrecy regarding council proceedings

- prescribed that Latin would be the only language that could be used at public sessions and most other meetings: "At the meetings of the council commissions, modern languages can also be used in addition to Latin, but subject to immediate translation into Latin."
- indicated how the discussion at the general sessions would proceed: introduction of the topic with a brief explanation, speeches for or against which must stick to the topic and not exceed ten minutes of length, voting on amendments, revision of the documents, resubmission of the total schema, more voting, eventual promulgation if it pleased the council fathers and the pope

Autumn, 1962 ▶ **The interior space of St. Peter's was prepared for the council.** The nave or interior of St. Peter's Basilica in Rome, as many readers know, has no permanent seats or pews. Instead—as in many large basilicas—the space is open and can accommodate a variety of seating arrangements. It is some 2,500 square meters (2734 square yards)—about half the size of a typical football or soccer field.

Background

This space was outfitted to provide some 2900 seats for council participants in addition to 200 more for the various *periti* (theological experts) who had been invited, and 130 for the Protestant, Anglican, Orthodox, and Jewish observers, guests of the council. These latter guests had the best views and most convenient seats in the basilica. It should be noted that the only women present in the council in the first two sessions were the wives of these guests. No Catholic women were present.

Coffee bars. Pope John also helped promote a more informal discussion than would have been possible in Latin by establishing two coffee bars adjoining the council hall in the basilica. These popular coffee shops came to be known during the council as Bar-Jonah and Bar-abas. It has been ascribed to Sr. Mary Luke Tobin[17], one of the first women who were eventually invited, that once they arrived, they should have called one of the coffee rooms, "Bar None."

In these rooms[18], which were each the size of a ballroom, the council fathers competed with the *periti*, the council guests, and their opponents in the debates, for the attention of the attendants to obtain their midmorning *cappuccino*. Here as well, less formal discussions could occur, and the participants could come to know one another in a context other than the official, Latin-dominated setting of the council sessions. Cigar smoking was allowed in these lounges, a sign of those times. And, of course, lavatories were also installed both inside and outside of the basilica.

The cost of outfitting this large nave was enormous for the church at that time. Many dioceses around the world sent special donations to help offset that cost. It is not inexpensive to conduct such a large meeting. Also, nearly half the bishops of the world could not afford the annual travel to and from Rome nor the lodgings in Rome for the council. Again, in his effort to make sure the entire world was represented, Pope John provided financial help from the Holy See.

Security. There was a fear that the council could be infiltrated by outside forces—such as communists—that would undermine its work. Therefore, around the entire perimeter of the official space in which the council would be conducted was established a security zone. The participants were made to pass through it each day, and each day they were also given their seating assignment for that day's general congregation. Seating was arranged according to the date of each one's appointment to the hierarchy rather than in national or regional groups. During the council, this changed somewhat because more than 250 council fathers died, and most were replaced.

Many bishops brought with them a priest secretary and a theologian who could help with the Latin translations. Altogether, as can be plainly seen, this was a complex and large enterprise. To ensure that everything was ready and was prepared according to his wishes, Pope John himself personally oversaw the work of preparing the basilica. He left nothing to chance.

September 5, 1962 ▶ (Only 5 weeks before the opening.) **Pope John issued** a *motu proprio* naming the heads of the ten council commissions that would oversee the preparation and presentation of the official schemas or discussion draft documents to be considered by the council. He also spelled out the council's rules and procedures and named a presiding council of ten cardinals from nine nations who would take turns presiding over council activities when the pope himself was not present.

Background

Among the rules was one that required a two-thirds majority for the enactment of council pronouncements. The pope wished to have as much unanimity as possible in council outcomes to add moral force to them.

The members of the curia had urged the pope to insist upon the use of Latin as the official language of the council. Of course, Latin was not the language of the Eastern rites nor of the Protestant, Anglican, Orthodox, or Jewish guests. It was not spoken on a day-to-day basis in most of the church. But it was the traditional language of church ritual and official texts. Nonetheless, it seemed strange to many observers that a council whose stated agenda was to update the church for the modern times would use a language that had not been modern for many centuries. But Latin it would be for its discourse and official documents.

Certain prelates, especially seminary professors, were able to speak Latin quite well and, therefore, rose as leaders quickly. They included Siri of Genoa, Italy, Suenens of Malines, Belgium, Doepfner of Munich, Germany, and Leger of Montreal, Canada. Others had to rely on their experts, known as *periti,* for translations because no translation equipment was provided to council fathers. Most could have used such help. It should be noted that the council guests did have translation equipment available to them, however.

It must have occurred to the council's organizers that no real debate would occur in Latin, and this would slow down or stop reform from moving forward. The papers presented in the council hall were formal, though brief. But council sessions were not usually the scene of much actual interchange. Only a few prelates in the world would have been capable of a sustained spontaneous discussion in Latin. The result of this Latinization of the council was, of course, that the real debates occurred elsewhere. Where?

By any measure, 2,500 cardinals, patriarchs, archbishops, and bishops, along with their staff, are a large number of guests. They could not lodge in the Vatican since only a small number of guest rooms are available there. So, they lived instead in a variety of settings all around the city of Rome. Colleges, monasteries, convents, retreat centers, and shrines hosted many visitors. In addition to the council fathers, hundreds of theologians and canon lawyers who worked as advisers to various bishops and conferences of bishops also needed lodging. Plus, there was also a massive press corps present, unlike any previous council. More than 1,000 reporters and photographers were present for the opening period.

After each day's formal general congregation, less formal gatherings occurred in these various residences around Rome. Here the participants could sort out the day's happenings, catch up on council gossip, and consider new ideas together. Short speeches were often given in these evening meetings, and various positions and strategies were discussed, amid vociferous debates, *all in the vernacular of the participants*. These evening meetings often included the residents of those places: seminarians, religious men and women, professors, lay Catholics, and other locals. Often these discussions spilled out of the chapels and refectories of these convents and seminaries and up onto the rooftops of Rome, famous for their views. A bit of wine or grappa may have found its way into those late-night rooftop discussions. These evening discussions often ended in a paper summarizing a position. These position papers were then translated into many of the world's major languages and shared among the other council participants. The essays sometimes had a significant influence on council outcomes.

As mentioned, the seating at the daily council congregations also did not lend itself to much dialogue. The seating plan had been prearranged by the organizers based purely on seniority, that is, on the order of appointment to the hierarchy. Participants were not seated by national groups and often may not have known the language of the prelate sitting to the left or right. But this stirring up of the bishops had the unforeseen effect of helping bishops from around the world meet each other and find common ground. For many, this was an unprecedented opportunity to talk with prelates from different parts of the world. In doing so, many discovered that they shared common goals for the church and suffered from common difficulties in carrying out practices first introduced 400 years earlier as a result of the council of Trent.

Daily General Congregations

Microphones were distributed throughout the nave of St. Peter's Basilica to allow for an orderly debate, although longer presentations were made from a central podium. No previous council had the use of microphones. Those who wished to speak, except for the cardinals, were required to make an application to the general secretary of the council beforehand.

Daily meetings—called "general congregations"—ran from 9:00 AM until around 12:15 PM. They began with Mass, celebrated each day in a different rite. There are some 18 rites of the church which are in union with Rome, but the Latin rite tended to dominate at the council because of its sheer size. Nonetheless, by celebrating Mass in the many varied rites of the church—some with married clergy, most in languages other than Latin, and many with customs that varied widely from the "Roman way of doing things," the bishops learned a valuable lesson. The Mass is the Mass, regardless of the language or custom of the rite. This helped open the door to reform of the liturgy in the Latin rite.

Following Mass, the Gospels were formally enthroned at the center of the nave, a sign to all that Scripture would play a significant role in the proceedings. Then there were announcements and scheduling matters so that the actual daily general congregations did not begin until about 10:15 AM each day. The daily general congregations were mainly given to speeches, first by the cardinals, followed by the bishops, and occasionally by *periti* or other guests. The full roster of scheduled speakers was seldom completed on any given day.

About 11:00 each morning, the scene in the basilica began to resemble that in most houses of parliament or congress as the fathers moved into the coffee bars nearby to visit and mingle. Loudspeakers there kept everyone informed of the proceedings, which were, after all, being conducted in Latin. When a ballot was announced, the prelates would scurry back to their seats for the vote.

Voting Procedures

In addition to speech-making, voting also occurred at these general congregations. The ballots were tabulated by a computer system designed for this use but employing "punch cards." Modern, high-speed computers were not available, but this was a significant improvement over whatever was used in any previous council.

Voting was a crucial part of the council's process. Votes were taken on a wide variety of matters in the debates, and one estimate is that more than 1.5 million ballots were cast during the four annual periods of the council. For most questions, a two-thirds majority was needed for passage.

Voting occurred for:

- The general sense of the council fathers regarding their first impressions of a schema, whether or not it should be used as the basis for discussion. Many schemas were returned for revision to the commissions responsible for preparing them before they were even discussed.
- When disagreement was evident about the general direction a document should take, the matter was placed before the council for a vote, asking, "Does it please the fathers that such and such be treated in this or that way?" The outcome of such voting gave direction to the various commissions responsible for incorporating revisions into the various schemas.
- Specific notions or ideas that might be included in a revision were also voted upon. Sometimes individual words or phrases were considered by vote. They were treated as amendments to the schema. These ideas could be attached to the ballot, and sometimes hundreds of them were attached for a single vote, creating significant challenges to the commissions and their staffs. These were known in Latin as *juxta modum* votes. With them, the council fathers voted "yes" but with an amendment. Voting on amendments gave direction to the commissions working on the revisions.
- Voting also occurred to end debate.
- When documents were nearing acceptability, voting occurred again, often resulting in additional amendment suggestions. This voting often took place chapter by chapter or even line by line.
- When the agreement was essentially reached, another penultimate vote was taken to send the document to the pope for promulgation.
- In the special sessions at which documents were actually

promulgated by the pope in the presence of the council fathers, a final vote was taken by way of affirmation.

- Finally, voting took place to bestow honors on various people or to show support for particular causes or events.

Applause was not permitted during the proceedings, but it often occurred and was used as an informal way of expressing the mind of the fathers on many matters.

As the pope had ordered, a council of ten presidents was chosen who would preside in turn over each day's work. Freedom of speech was assured, but addresses were tightly limited to ten minutes and to the topic at hand. Anyone who strayed from these limits was gently but firmly interrupted and asked to stay on task or to end his remarks if they'd grown too long.

September 11, 1962 ▶ **Pope John addressed the world**, asking for prayers for the council.

Early September, 1962 ▶ The bishops of the world arrive in Rome for the beginning of the council itself. With all this preparation completed, the day finally arrived for travel to Rome. In chanceries, monasteries, and universities all over the world, bishops, abbots, and theologians began their journeys. They packed up their vestments, books, and council agendas and headed to the Eternal City.

Background

As mentioned, many of the world's bishops traveled to the council accompanied by small groups of staff members to assist them with translation and research. Some of the Germans are even said to have brought their own printing presses to Rome, apparently aware of the lack of any Italian sense of urgency when deadlines were involved. Having translators and presses handy would allow them to make translations of the Latin documents as well as various theological position papers widely available in the City of Rome to facilitate the adoption of reforms.

Indeed, this council would undertake important questions that had been before the church for many, many centuries without open discussion:

- the role of bishops in their relationship to the bishop of Rome
- the place and role of lay people in the life and operations of

the church
- the understanding and place of religious liberty in the modern church and world
- the church's teaching on divine revelation and its source
- the church's attitude toward and desire for a better relationship with the Jews, especially in light of the Holocaust which had occurred within everyone's memory
- the way Christian unity would be approached
- the reform and restoration of the liturgy, the catechumenate, the diaconate, religious life, and the role of the laity
- and most remarkably and without precedence, the place and relationship of the church to the whole modern world, with all its new challenges and needs, including its place in the lives of all people: Catholics, other Christians, non-Christians, nonbelievers, and all people of goodwill.

The Second Vatican Council was now set to begin.

The First Annual Period
September to December 1962

October 11, 1962 ▶ **The first of what would become four periods or annual gatherings got underway** with Pope John's opening address to the council. The first session ran until December 8, 1962.

The Opening Procession

Early on the morning of Thursday, October 11, 1962, a large crowd had gathered in the piazza of St. Peter's in Vatican City. People had come from every corner of the world to witness this historic moment. The crowd waited to observe a religious event so grand in scale and so unusual that few could have understood entirely what they were about to see.

It was on this day that the windows of the church were thrown open by Pope John XXIII. They were thrown open so that fresh breezes and light could burst into the chambers, long darkened by a too-rigid and too-triumphal application of the decrees of the Council of Trent and the long period following it. Likewise, the windows and doors of the church had been nailed shut by the steady growth of papal power and general clericalism in the church, primarily as it defended itself from the French Revolution, the Enlightenment, and the fear of modern thought. The response of the church to these social forces was to strengthen the center: the papacy. It did this by asserting its authority through numerous encyclicals and defensive decisions from the 1830s onward to the eve of Vatican II, the period from Popes Gregory XVI to Pius XII.

During these defensive years, the church outrightly condemned freedom of conscience, religious liberty of any kind, social change, reconciliation to modern forms of thought, democracy, freedom of the press, any conversation about reform in the church, the use of vernacular in the liturgy, ecumenism in any form, modern biblical study, and birth control.[19] All of these topics (except birth control!) eventually found their way onto the agenda at Vatican II—fresh air and new light indeed!

Everyone standing there in the piazza that morning must have been stirred when a somewhat cloudy and wet night gave way at precisely 8:00 AM to bright Roman sunlight in the piazza. At that precise hour, two papal guards in dress uniforms slowly drew open the doors to the papal apartments on the north side of the square. These massive bronze doors stand at the head of Bernini's *Scala Regia*—the staircase leading to the apartment of the pope. Behind these doors stood row upon row of bishops, patriarchs, archbishops, abbots, and scarlet-clad cardinals, all under the command of the papal master of ceremonies. They were poised to descend the stair. The whole spectacle must have resembled some medieval Byzantine ceremony.

They marched out of the Vatican palace eight-abreast, down into the well-guarded square, a seemingly endless number of them, more than 2,500 in all! Beneath their miters or other head-dresses, their faces were the colors of the world. More than 500 of them were from South America, 126 were native Asians, 118 were native Africans. (At Vatican I, only 55 of the attendees were not European, and none of them was native Asian or African.)

Slowly they moved across the square, swinging to the right as they moved out of the staircase, then right again to mount the vast, sprawling steps of the basilica.

Finally, the pope appeared, John XXIII. He was being carried on the ancient platform used for special occasions, the *sedi gestatoria,* waving warmly in response to the acclamation of the crowd. He offered them his blessing. He smiled as he was moved through them and wept quietly. What must have been his thoughts that day? What must have he borne in his heart as this event unfolded, initially against the wishes of all his Vatican advisers?

No one in the crowd or the procession, including the Holy Father himself, could have known that this council would last through four annual periods with 168 daily sessions (called general congregations) spread over that time. More than 2,000 speeches would be given. More than 4,000 amendments would be offered to the documents. And more than 1.5 million ballots would be cast as the council fathers decided nearly 700 separate questions about the matters before them.

Pope John's Opening Address
The prelates celebrated the Mass of the Holy Spirit, chanting the readings in both Latin and Greek to signify the unity of East and

West. Then the pope delivered his sermon, a keynote that would set the tone and agenda for the council. In clear, resonant Latin that was well-heard throughout the basilica, he said he was tired of listening to the negative tones of his advisors. "Though burning with zeal," he said, "they are not endowed with very much sense of discretion or measure." These, the pope said, believe that our modern times, compared to past ages in the church, are somehow worse, and he said, "they behave as though they had learned nothing from history, which is nevertheless the great teacher of life."

"We feel that we must disagree with these prophets of doom, who are always forecasting disaster as though the end of the world were at hand," the pope added.

With these opening words, Pope John XXIII gave perspective to much that had gone on during the preparation period of the council. Seated there with him were the very doomsayers he was describing: Cardinal Ottaviani (seated at his immediate right hand), Cardinals Siri and Ruffini, Pericle Felici, Enrico Dante (papal master of ceremonies), and many others. Even though acting in good faith, these had been the obstructionists during the preparatory period, and they must have felt the heat of the pope's words as they sat there that day. As he went on to outline his intentions for the council, they must have wondered where this would lead.

The Holy Father left no doubt about that.

"Divine Providence," the pope continued, "is leading us to a new order of human relations." How well this pope knew that. How well this comment reflected the newly emerging life of the modern church where bishops were pastors rather than bureaucrats or legal experts. It's time, the pope went on to say, for the church "to bring herself up to date where required." His wishes were clear; there would be *aggiornamento* in the church.

Aggiornamento is an Italian word that has come to signify that throwing open of the church's windows (which I alluded to above) to allow reform and freshness to replace all that has grown stale. It means, more literally in Italian, to make things ready for today, today's needs, today's times, today's people.

Pope John went on to say that he had not called the council so that a new doctrine or dogma could be defined. A council, he said, would not be necessary for that. Instead, he said, "the world ex-

pects a step forward toward doctrinal penetration and the formation of conscience," and this work would proceed by employing
methods of research and literary forms of modern thought.

"The substance of the ancient doctrine" of the faith is one thing,
he said, "the way in which it is expressed is another." With this,
he called for new ways of teaching the truths of the faith and for
a contemporary language to express the truth. Such a new language, of course, would never be adequate, just as past attempts
at expressing the truth had not been. But an updated way of expressing our faith would fit these times more appropriately.

The pope explicitly declared that this council would not include
the condemnation of anyone. "Nowadays, the Bride of Christ
prefers to make use of the medicine of mercy rather than that of
severity," he explained. "She considers that she meets the needs
of the present day by demonstrating the validity of her teaching
rather than by condemnation."

John concluded by speaking about the unity of the human
family. The key, he said, to such unity, including not only Christians but "those who follow non-Christian religions," would be
love—"the fullness of charity," as he put it.

**The pope's inaugural address marked the end of a period of
intransigence and rigidity in the church.** It opened the doors of
the church to renewal and reform. It heartened the leaders of this
reform while at the same time it made possible the open debates
which characterized Vatican II. It prevented the council from
focusing on the definition of new doctrine or condemnation of
error, on which all previous councils had concentrated. From that
point forward, the work of the council belonged to the bishops,
and following this address, the pope did not enter the hall again
until the end of the first period.

It has been said that in the long history of the church, there
have been many significant speeches. Think of Peter's sermon
on the first Pentecost. Or think of Stephen before he was stoned.
In that long ecclesial history, Pope John's opening speech at the
Second Vatican Council surely takes its place among the top five
or ten most significant addresses. It announced a new Pentecost.
And like, Stephen, it invited all within its hearing to be less stiff-
necked and less opposed to the Holy Spirit moving in our midst
(Acts 7:51).

Pope John XXIII's Opening
Speech at the Second Vatican Council
October 11, 1962

Paraphrased

The entire church rejoices today
　　　　because that longed-for moment
　　　　has finally arrived when,
　　　　　　　under the watchful eye
　　　　　　　of the Virgin Mother of God,
　　　　the Second Vatican Council is opened,
　　　　　　　here beside the tomb of St. Peter.
The previous ecumenical councils of the church,
　　　　some 20 in number,
　　　　plus many other regional ones,
　　　　all prove clearly the vigor
　　　　　　　of the Catholic Church
　　　　　　　and are recorded as shining lights
　　　　　　　in the church's history.

In calling this particular council,
　　　　I assert once again the church's
　　　　enduring authority to teach the Faith,
　　　　and I hope that in these times,
　　　　　　　filled with needs and opportunities
　　　　　　　as well as errors,
　　　　the church's teachings will be presented
　　　　　　　exceptionally well to all people.

It is natural for us to look back into our history
　　　　and listen again to the voices of leaders,
　　　　both in the East and the West,
　　　　where, beginning in the fourth century,
　　　　　　　councils like this have gathered.
But despite the joys of these previous councils,
　　　　there has also been a trail of sorrow and trial,
　　　　just as Simeon foretold to Mary
　　　　　　　that Jesus would be the source
　　　　　　　of both the fall and the rise of many.

What confronts the church today is not new:
    those who know Jesus who is the Christ enjoy light,
      goodness,
      order,
      and peace.
Those who oppose Jesus the Christ sink into confusion,
    bitter human relations,
    and the constant danger of war.

Ecumenical councils like this, whenever they gather,
    are an occasion for the celebration once again
    of the unity between Jesus and the church.
They lead to a clearer announcement of the truth,
    to guidance for people in everyday life,
    and to the strengthening of spiritual energy
      for goodness' sake.
We now stand in the wake of 20 centuries
    of such history as we begin.
For the sake of the historical record,
    let me mention the first moment
    when the idea of calling such a council
      first came to me.
I first uttered the words on January 25, 1959,
    on the feast of the Conversion of St. Paul,
    in the church dedicated to him in Rome.
It was completely unexpected,
    like a flash of heavenly light,
    and it gave rise to three years
      of tremendous activity
      throughout the world
      in preparation for this day.
These years alone have been an initial gift of grace.
I confidently trust that under the light of this council
    the church will become richer
    in spiritual matters
      and, with this new energy,
      will look to the future without fear.
In fact, by bringing itself up-to-date where needed,
    the church will make people, families,
    and whole nations

really turn their minds toward divine things.
And, therefore, we are all very grateful for this moment.

Moreover, I also want to mention
  before you now my own assessment
  of the happy circumstances
  under which this council begins its work.
As I go about my daily work as pope,
  I sometimes have to listen, with much regret,
   to voices of persons who,
   though burning with zeal,
    are not endowed with too much sense
     of discretion or measure.
These people can see nothing but a decline of truth
  and the ruin of the church
  in these modern times.
They say that our era, in comparison with past ones,
  is getting worse,
  and they behave as though
  they had learned nothing from history,
  which is, nonetheless, the teacher of life.
They behave as though at the time of former councils,
  everything was a full triumph
  for the Christian idea and religious liberty.
I feel I must disagree with these prophets of gloom
  who are always forecasting disaster
  as though the end of the world was at hand.

In fact, at the present time,
  Divine Providence is leading us
  to a new order of human relations which,
   by the very effort of the people of this time,
   is directed toward the fulfillment
    of God's great plans for us.
Everything, even human differences,
  leads to a greater good for the church.

It's easy to see this
  if you look even casually through history.
Most of the councils called in the past
  were forced to address

serious challenges to the church brought about
      by civil authorities.
Most of the world today does not live
      under such civil tyranny,
      and this is a great thing.
I am saddened, of course,
      by those places where oppression still exists,
      and indeed, some bishops are notable here today
      mainly by their absence
         where they are imprisoned for their Faith.
And even though modern life brings with it
      great stress and pressure
      from economic and political sides,
         nonetheless, it at least has the advantage
         of having freed the church
            from obstacles to its freedom
            in most parts of the world.

The greatest concern of this council is this:
      that the sacred and central truths
      of our Christian faith
      should be guarded and taught more effectively.
These central truths embrace the whole human person,
      composed as we are of body and soul,
      and since we're pilgrims on earth,
         they lead us always toward heaven.
This puts into perspective that we are to use earthly things
      only to attain a divine good.
According to the sixth chapter of the Gospel of Matthew,
      Jesus called on us to seek first the Reign of God,
         addressing our energy to that.
But Jesus also completed that thought by saying that,
      if we did seek that first,
      all worldly things would be given to us as well.
Both sides of this equation are present today,
      as they have always been,
      and we take this into account as we begin.

In this effort, we will not depart from the truth
      as it is passed on to us

by the early Fathers of the church.
But we will also be attentive to these times,
    to the new conditions and new forms of life
        present in the modern world
           which have opened new arenas of work
              for Catholics.
So, while the church is mindful
    of marvelous human progress,
    it is also eager to remind people
    that God is the real source of wisdom and beauty.

Having said this, it is clear that much
    is expected of us here
    regarding the passing on
        of the doctrines of the church.
We have done this without fail for 20 centuries,
    despite occasional difficulties in that regard.
The important point of this council is not, therefore,
    a discussion of one article or another
    of the fundamental teachings of the church;
    a council would not be needed for such work.
Instead, the work of this council is to better articulate
    the doctrine of the church for this age.
This doctrine should be studied and expounded
    through the methods of research
    and literary forms of modern thought.
Here is a crucial distinction on which our work is based:
    The *substance* of our central beliefs is one thing,
    and *the way in which it is presented* is another.
It is this latter presentation of the faith
    with which we are concerned here
        and our approach to this
        will be a thoroughly pastoral one.

As we open this council we see, as always,
    that the truth of Jesus is permanent.
Often, as one age succeeds another,
    the opinions of people follow one another
    and exclude each other.
Errors creep in but vanish like fog before the sun.

In the past, we have opposed these errors
   and often condemned them.
But today we prefer to make use of the medicine of mercy
      rather than that of severity.
We meet the needs of the present day
         by demonstrating the validity of our teachings
         rather than by condemning others.
In fact, error today is so apparent when it emerges
      that people themselves reject it.
People are ever more convinced
      of the high dignity of the human person,
      the evil of violence,
      and the dead-end of the arms race,
      and political domination.

That being so, the Catholic Church in this council
         desires to show herself as the loving mother of all:
            benign,
            patient,
            full of mercy and goodness
            toward all who are separated from her.
The church does not offer riches that will pass away
      to the people of today.
Like Peter when he was asked for alms,
      we say that we have neither silver nor gold
         but that we have a power in Jesus, who is the Christ
            to offer the world: a way to walk in truth.
We distribute the goods of divine grace to all people
      and this raises the children of God to great dignity.
We open here the fountain of our life-giving doctrines
      which allows all people to understand
      their real dignity and purpose.
Finally, through our members,
      we spread Christian charity,
      the most powerful tool
      in eliminating the seeds of discord
            and in establishing harmony,
               peace, and unity.

True peace and salvation are associated with having
    a complete grasp of revealed truth.
This truth is passed on through the doctrines of the church,
    and the church wishes very much
    to promote and defend this truth
        so that everyone can have access to it
        with a unity of understanding.
Unfortunately, the whole Christian family does not have
    this unity of mind.
The Catholic Church considers it a duty to work actively
    to bring about that unity,
    which Jesus himself called for
        in his final prayers.
It is a triple sort of unity that we seek.

First, a unity among Catholics themselves
    which we want to keep firm and strong.
Second, a unity of prayer and desire
    among those other Christians
    now separated from Rome.
And third, a unity in esteem and respect
    for those who follow non-Christian religions.

It is the clear aim of this council
    to bring together the church's best energies
    and to strive to have people welcome favorably
        the good tidings of salvation.
This council will prepare and consolidate
    the path toward that unity of humankind
    which is required as a necessary foundation
    so that the earthly city
    may be brought to resemble the heavenly one
        where truth reigns,
        charity is the law,
        and eternity is the timetable.

In conclusion, I direct my voice to you,
    my venerable fellow bishops of the church.
We are gathered here today in this great Vatican basilica
    upon which the history of the church is hinged,
        where heaven and earth are closely joined,

near the tomb of Peter and so many others
who have gone before us in faith.
The council now beginning rises in the church
like daybreak,
a forerunner of most splendid light.
It is now only dawn.
And already, at this first announcement
of the rising day,
how much sweetness fills our heart!
Everything here breathes sanctity and arouses great joy.
The church is now in your hands,
gathered as you are here
from all the continents of the world.
We might say that heaven and earth
are united in the holding of this council,
the saints of heaven to protect us
and the people on earth
looking for inspiration and guidance.
Indeed, our work is expected to correspond
to the modern needs
of the various peoples of the world.
This requires of you serenity of mind,
brotherly concord,
moderation in proposals,
dignity in discussion,
and wisdom of deliberation.
God grant that your labors and work,
toward which the eyes of all people
and desires of the entire world are turned,
may generously fulfill the hopes of all.

Almighty God!
In you we place all our confidence,
not trusting in our own strength.
Look down kindly on these pastors of your church.
May the light of your grace help us
in making decisions
and in making laws.
Graciously hear the prayers which we offer you
with unanimity of faith, voice, and mind.

O Mary, help of Christians, help of bishops,
    arrange all things for a happy outcome.
With your spouse, St. Joseph;
    the holy apostles, Peter and Paul;
    St. John the Baptist; and St. John the Evangelist
      intercede to God for us.
Jesus, you are the Christ and our loving redeemer,
    immortal ruler of people and the ages,
      be love,
      be power,
      and be glory forever and ever. Amen.

The Work of the First Period of the Council
1962

October 13, 1962 ▶ Two days later, the council met in its first general congregation but adjourned after only an hour, following **the motion by Cardinal Lienart** (from the Archdiocese of Lille in France), seconded by Cardinal Frings (from the Archdiocese of Cologne in Germany), to allow the bishops to gather as national groups in order to better consider who would best be chosen for the 160 posts open in the ten commissions which would steer the council debates. The motion met with sustained and loud applause in the council hall. It should be noted that applause of this sort was not approved by the rules. Nonetheless, the idea won the day, and the first general congregation adjourned before 10:00 AM. This was seen as a blow to the leaders of the group of more cautious bishops who feared reform and who had hoped to have their handpicked choices for these seats approved.

Background

It should be noted that the so-called "conservative party" at the council was composed of council fathers from many parts of the world, including many working in the Roman Curia. This curia is comprised of various congregations and offices which assist the pope in the worldwide administration of the church. Many of the leaders of this curia were opposed to the reforms being proposed because they believed the church was adequately meeting the demands of the gospel in its pre-Vatican II form.

We must always remember that everyone at the council acted in good faith for what they believed sincerely was right for the church. As we read the story of the council, we must bear in mind that there were no "good guys" or "bad guys" at Vatican II. Everyone present was a fellow Catholic acting in good faith and exercising his conscience. Some bishops of the world—and this turned out to be an 85 or 90% majority—were unafraid of reform and ready to see the church enact it. Others—a smaller but still faithful minority—were more cautious about such reform.

Nonetheless, the effect of the move by the bishops to assert their control on this process of choosing members of the commissions was tremendous. The council showed, first of all, that it could act decisively.

Secondly, the caucusing that followed provided a learning period for all the council fathers because, as lists were drawn up and attempts made to provide for adequate international representation, the discussions were intense. This period fused the participants into a real working body, and the outcome was considered by most to be a fair representation of the church's complexion.

Thirdly, this action by such a unanimous consent of the council fathers also sent a signal to the world, to the press, and to everyone else in the room that this council would not be a rubber stamp of the wishes of the Roman Curia at the center of the church—even though they were known to act in good faith—but that the council "belonged to the bishops of the world."

October 13, 1962 ▶ **800 journalists from around the world met with Pope John** who urged them to present the council's proceedings fairly and accurately. He promised them his cooperation. He also urged them to avoid the sensational and to report on the substantial aspects of the council. "We felt keenly that we must tell you personally how much we desire your loyal cooperation in presenting this great event in its true colors," he told them.

On the same day ▶ The pope spoke to the 35 observers and guests representing **17 Orthodox, Protestant, and Anglican denominations** who attended the first period of the council in 1962. "It is now for the Catholic Church to bend herself to her work with calmness and generosity," he told them. "It is for you to observe her with renewed and friendly attention."

October 16, 1962 ▶ **The schema on the liturgy** was chosen as the first item with which the council would deal. The council fathers passed over other possible first-choice schemas because they seemed unready.

Background

It is important to note that **the liturgical renewal succeeded as it did** in the face of a well-organized, top-down fight against "modernism" because it occurred in league with the growth of biblical study, enhanced no doubt by Pius XII's *Divino Afflante Spiritu* in 1943. Patristic studies were well underway in Europe as well, along with a strong and carefully enacted ecumenical movement. The liturgical movement was theologically well-grounded in part because of the recovery of St. Paul's doctrine that the Church is "the mystical body of Jesus who is the Christ," the *ressourcement* of which originated in Tübingen in the nineteenth century.

The liturgical movement began, one could say, in 1909 at a Catholic congress in Belgium, led by a former labor chaplain and Benedictine monk, Lambert Beauduin OSB. Later, Beauduin mentored Virgil Michel OSB from St. John's Abbey in Collegeville, Minnesota, a visible and articulate leader of the American liturgical renewal movement. Fr Joseph Komonchak[20] points out that Beauduin had also been a friend of Angelo Roncalli for many years, including during Roncalli's time serving in Paris as nuncio to France. Komonchak quotes Thomas Stransky who wrote the forward to Sonya A. Quitslund's book, *Beauduin, A Prophet Vindicated*[21], saying that there was one report that "during their frequent private evenings together in Paris, when the future pope was nuncio to France, the two of them fantacized [sic] about the need and possibility of another ecumenical council."

October 20, 1962 ▶ **The council's first act** was to send a "message to the world," calling for peace and social justice for all humankind. "We wish to convey to all people and to all nations the message of salvation, love, and peace which Jesus brought to the world and entrusted to the church," the message began.

October 22, 1962 ▶ **The schema** (draft document) **on the liturgy was introduced** for debate. The official council press office reported that this was the first topic because the council's work would be directed primarily toward the task of the internal renewal of the church. The debate was wide-ranging, including suggestions for the use of the vernacular, more varied use of Scripture, communion under both forms, and concelebration. The discussion on the liturgy lasted through fifteen general congregations, ending on November 13. The council fathers proposed 625 amendments to the original schema.

On the same day ▶ Pope John raised the status of **the Secretariat for Christian Unity** to the level of an official commission, signaling his commitment to ecumenism. Cardinal Augustin Bea SJ remained its head.

November 14, 1962 ▶ **The schema on sources of divine revelation** was introduced by Cardinal Ottaviani for debate under the name "On the Sources of Revelation." The debates which followed demonstrated that this schema, insisting as it did on the status quo, did not meet the needs of the modern church. A tense week of speeches and drama followed.

On the same day ▶ **The schema on liturgy** came to its first significant vote to determine whether, in substance, it adequately represented what the council fathers wanted. It passed with only a handful of negative votes: 2,162 to 46! This was a significant victory for those who favored liturgical updating and a clear sign to the waiting world that this council would indeed undertake real reform and not merely affirm the status quo.

November 20, 1962 ▶ **The debate on divine revelation** was halted amid a growing consensus that the schema as originally presented did not adequately address the needs of the day or the spirit of Pope John in calling the council in the first place. "What then did the pope have in mind?" Cardinal Bea, the feeble but brilliant leader of the Secretariat for Christian Unity, asked. He had in mind, the cardinal said, "that the faith of the church should be presented in all its integrity and purity, but in such a manner that it will be received today with goodwill. For we are shepherds," he went on to say. "What our times demand is a pastoral approach, demonstrating the love and kindness that flow from our religion." It was Cardinal Bea's voice, but the sentiments of John XXIII and everyone knew it.

A vote was taken to determine whether the schema as it stood should be returned to its drafting commission for revisions. **The vote failed** to reach the two-thirds majority required by the rules but in a historic move, Pope John himself intervened and sent the schema to a specially designed commission for revision. This was another blow for the more cautious bishops who feared reform at the council.

November 23, 1962 ▶ The schema on **the modern means of communications** for preaching the gospel to all and spreading the principles of justice, peace, and human dignity was introduced.

November 26, 1962 ▶ The schema on communications was approved mostly as it was presented. Council work moved on to what were considered more critical matters, including the promotion of greater unity between Roman and Eastern Christians. It should be noted that the document on communications was written before the advent of personal computers, mobile phones, the internet, or any other forms of modern communication and, therefore, is somewhat out-of-date today.

November 27, 1962 ▶ The first lay observer was invited to the council, Jean Guitton, a member of the French Academy whom Pope John knew when he lived in Paris as papal nuncio to France. It should be noted that no Catholic women had yet been invited to take part in the council.

November 30, 1962 ▶ The schema on the unity of Roman and Eastern Catholic Churches was defeated 2,068 to 36, with 8 invalid ballots. It was generally seen as inadequate to address the situation facing the modern church. The matter would have to be addressed again later. It later appeared as a chapter in the Decree on Ecumenism before the bishops eventually drafted a decree on the Eastern Catholic Churches.

It should be noted that the Western or Latin church includes **five liturgical traditions spread among 23 Eastern Catholic Churches** plus the Latin rite common in the West for a total of six. These include: (1) the Alexandrian Rite, (2) the Armenian Rite, (3) the Byzantine Rite, (4) the East Syriac Rite, and (5) the West Syriac Rite. These 23 churches follow Oriental Canon Law, which notably allows for a married clergy, among other differences. The churches of the East did not pass through the Reformation and other shaping forces with which the West had had to deal.

The Greek and Russian Orthodox churches are not in union with the Western or Latin church but attended the council as observers.

December 1, 1962 ▶ The schema on the church was introduced for debate by Cardinal Alfredo Ottaviani, chair of the Theological Commission which had prepared it. Many council fathers felt that this document's topic should be the focus of the council as a whole. It was long-awaited because the cardinal held it up as he sought a suitable way to present it to the council fathers. It was distributed only at the last minute so that participants did not have time to read it before it was presented. By and large, Ottaviani's commission prepared a draft that hailed the status quo as acceptable and did not address the church as the people of God. It was called *De Ecclesia*. Ottaviani's presentation was peevish and aggressive, according to Yves Congar OP[22]. The cardinal complained that an alternative schema was already circulating, even before this one was presented, which was true. The document was very long—some 82 pages in length—and seemed preoccupied with obedience to ecclesiastical authority.

Early December 1962 ▶ **The debate on the schema on the church got underway.** Cardinal Alfrink of the Archdiocese of Utrecht in the Netherlands called for a new schema to be drafted. Cardinal Ritter of the Archdiocese of St. Louis in the United States echoed that call. But it was Archbishop De Smedt of the Diocese of Bruges in Belgium who dealt a severe blow to this document's chances. He said it was full of triumphalism, clericalism, and juridicism. He said the style was pompous and out of touch with the reality of today's people. We must beware, he said, of falling into some sort of bishop or pope worship. The church must be our mother, not our judge, he said. And so, the debate raged on.

December 4, 1962 ▶ **Cardinal Suenens**—in what became a real turning point in the entire council—rose and spoke in favor of redrafting **the schema on the church.** As Vatican I was the council of the papacy, he said, let this be the council of the church of Jesus who is the Christ, the light of nations! He went on to propose that the document be divided into two parts: one dealing with the nature of the church itself, *ad intra* as it were, and the other dealing with the church's mission in the world, *ad extra* as it were. He called on the church to be in dialogue with the society around it on matters such as the dignity of the human person, social justice, private property, the poor, internal peace within nations, and international relations. It was his stress on dialogue that became a leitmotif for the rest of the council. His speech was met with sustained applause, so much so that it had to be choked off by the day's president with a reminder that such boisterous responses were not in order.

Cardinal Bea seconded Suenens' remarks, followed by others who agreed, along with a smaller number who favored the approach taken by Ottaviani's commission.

December 5, 1962 ▶ **Cardinal Giovanni Battista Montini of Milan** rose to take the microphone. In the entire first session, he addressed the council only twice. He said that he approved wholeheartedly of Cardinal Suenens' statement of the day before regarding the need for revision of the document on the church and confirmed the suspicion in the council that Suenens has indeed been speaking the mind and heart of Pope John himself. The church, Montini went on to say, is nothing by itself. It is not so much that the church has Jesus as the Christ, he said, but that Jesus has the church to carry on his work of bringing salvation to all. It was up to this council, he said, to clearly restate "the mind and will of Christ" by defining collegiality among bishops, projecting a truly ecumenical view of the church, and teaching faithfully that each bishop is indeed a vicar of Jesus.

It is necessary, he said, to send this schema back to its commission for redrafting. All present knew that he was speaking for Pope John. It should be noted that Montini was the only cardinal who had been invited to reside in the papal apartments as Pope John's houseguest during the eight weeks of the first period[23]. Only a few months later, this very cardinal, Giovanni Montini, was named Pope Paul VI.

December 6, 1962 ▶ Pope John ordered that, between periods, all **the schemas were to be reworked** by various commissions and sent to the bishops of the world for their comment. To coordinate this effort, **he created a new central commission**, which included Cardinals Lienart, Urbani, Spellman, Confalonieri, Doepfner, and Suenens. The pope ordered the commission to consult theological experts on a wide scale. All of this was yet another severe setback for the more cautious bishops who feared reform at the council.

December 7, 1962 ▶ The council approved **the first chapter of the document on the liturgy** with 1,922 "yes" votes, 180 "yes with reservations" votes, 11 "no" votes, and 5 invalid ballots. The chapter allowed specific changes to update the Mass, including the use of vernacular languages and a more participatory rite.

The chapter contained the fundamental principles which the following chapters would elaborate. Those principles would also be called into play with many of the following documents in periods two, three, and four of the council. The church's sacramental and prayer life was moved to center stage in this act, but it was a blow for the more cautious bishops who feared reform at the council.

On this same day ▶ **Pope John visited the council** for the first time since its opening to thank the members for their work and for their generosity and kindness toward one another.

December 8, 1962 ▶ **The first period of the Second Vatican Council was formally adjourned** for nine months, until September 8, 1963. In his address, the pope stressed that he appreciated the sometimes sharply divergent views expressed in the first period because this demonstrated the "holy liberty" of thought in the church. "A good beginning has been made," he said. It should be noted that, even though no formal documents were approved in this first session, three of the four constitutions that would eventually be promulgated were introduced, and one of them, the constitution on the liturgy, received a nearly unanimous test approval. The two others, those dealing with the church and divine revelation, were examined carefully and were on track for further work in the next period that would occur in the fall of 1963. And perhaps most importantly, the council fathers left Rome with a sense of the way forward for the council.

The Interim Between Annual Periods 1 and 2 & the Death of Pope John XXIII
December 1962 to September 1963

During March ▶ **Pope John established a commission** to study questions related to birth control. It should be noted that there was a great hesitancy on the part of both popes, John and Paul, to allow this matter to be decided by the council fathers. The council fathers were not told about this commission until late June of the following year, 1964.

During April ▶ Pope John, already suffering from the final stages of painful stomach cancer, **published a pivotal encyclical on human rights and world peace, entitled** *Pacem in Terris.*

June 3, 1963 ▶ **Pope John XXIII died.**

Background

It was a public matter that Pope John was very sick and on the verge of death. Such a public death was rare for popes, but John was a rare man. As news of his impending death went out, large crowds gathered in St. Peter's Square, praying and weeping, waiting, and praying. In the middle of the night passing to June 3, Pope John awoke and said twice with great emphasis, "Lord, you know that I love you." These were his last distinct words. He was preparing to die. The crowd in St. Peter's, as if under a spell, grew larger yet. The world media was there within the vigil. Everyone present was swept up in the power of this gentle man from Bergamo, this funny and kind man, this noble churchman drawn from farmers[24].

A large outdoor Mass began in the piazza at 5:00 PM on June 3. The throng began to pray, people of every faith on earth, people who felt that they had known this man personally. His loss was personal, not ecclesial. In John, they had an advocate. If you were poor, he took your part. If you were outside the church, he opened wide his arms to love you. Even if you were an atheist, he offered you his friendship. If you were rejected, he took you in.

The crowd in the piazza grew quiet and prayerful as Cardinal Traglia presided at Mass. It was as though two sacrifices were being enacted simultaneously: that of John, the servant of the servants of God, alongside the sacrifice of Jesus who is the Christ. At that time in the Mass, a "Last Gospel" was proclaimed after the communion rite. Cardinal Traglia said the words in Latin: *Fuit homo missus a Deo, cui nomen erat Joannes* (John 1:6). "There was a man sent from God whose name was John." Heaven and earth seemed to come together to welcome Pope John home, for at that very moment, he was taking his final breath.

At his bedside were farmers and cardinals: the story of his life. The members of his family were present, Monsignor Capovilla who had been his friend and trusted secretary, his doctors, and the nuns from Bergamo who had been his housekeepers. At 7:45 PM, the Mass being celebrated in St. Peter's Square came to an end with the audible *Ita missa est* (it is ended). Everyone in the now-silent bed-chamber of the dying man could hear those words through the open June window of the Vatican. Pope John gave a last faint rattle. His breathing became very weak, then stopped altogether. It was 7:49 PM, June 3rd, 1963. Pope John XXIII was dead.

He was mourned by the entire world, which seemed to understand that it had lost a man of great vision and compassion. A conclave followed immediately.[25]

June 21, 1963 ▶ Giovanni Montini was elected pope and took the name, **Pope Paul VI.**

June 22, 1963 ▶ **Pope Paul announced his intention to continue the ecumenical council.** He announced the opening date for the second annual period would be on September 29, 1963—sooner than had been expected by even the most optimistic observer since preparations had stopped upon the death of Pope John.

June 23, 1963 ▶ From the window of the papal library, Pope Paul introduced his friend and confidant—**Cardinal Suenens**—to a cheering crowd. This is significant because Cardinal Suenens played such a central role in moving reforms forward in the council. His presence was a sign that the new pope would continue the program of his predecessor.

September 15, 1963 ▶ Pope Paul announced the formation of **a steering committee** to direct the work of the second period. The members of the committee were three bishops who favored more reform (Cardinals Suenens, Doepfner, and Lercaro) and one moderate (Agagianian).

September 21, 1963 ▶ **Pope Paul delivered an address to members of the curia** and other Vatican workers in which he clearly and tactfully expressed every theme of reform that had been raised by the bishops who favored more reform in the first period. He called on the curia to be faithful to his wishes and made himself perfectly clear by referring to himself as "the pope who today has made the legacy of Pope John his own and has also made it a program for the entire church..." He discussed the need to update the curia itself by using Pope John's word, *aggiornamento,* and then said, simply, "Various reforms are therefore necessary."

The Second Annual Period
September to December 1963

September 29, 1963 ▶ **The second period of the council opened.** Pope Paul invited 63 separated Christian observers and 11 Catholic laymen (but still no Catholic women) to attend this session, an increase over the first session. The pope opened this session with a long and stirring speech, addressing the "living presence" of Pope John and committing himself to continued reform. In his opening address, Pope Paul set the stage for the rest of the council.

1. **He recalled the spirit of John XXIII**, quoted him, and embraced *aggiornamento* as his own program for reform. He pointed out that the church needed reform, not because it had strayed, but in order to keep up with the times.

2. **He embraced Christian unity as his own goal**. The pope called the process of re-establishing Christian unity the council's "spiritual drama." At that point, he turned to the separated Christians seated within his sight and told them that if we are in any way to blame for this separation, we humbly beg God's forgiveness and ask pardon, too, of our brethren who feel they have been injured by us. For our part, he said, we willingly forgive the injuries which the Catholic Church has suffered.

3. **He also said he wanted the church to engage in dialogue** with the contemporary world. The pope said that the council fathers should no longer be concerned only "to conduct a dialogue" among themselves, "but rather to open one with the world."

October 1, 1963 ▶ **The revised schema on the nature of the church** was distributed to the council fathers. They now took up **the debate on this matter** once again with the overwhelming approval of the assembly. The vote to proceed based on the revised schema was 2,231 to 43, with 27 invalid ballots. The revised schema included a greater emphasis on the church as mystery, on the church as first and foremost the people of God, on the call to holiness, and on other changes desired by the council fathers.

Background

The revised schema opened with the memorable words, *Lumen Gentium cum sit Christus*. The Constitution eventually took its name from this line, which means in English, "Christ is the light of the nations." It should be noted that this differs from earlier versions, which may have said that the church is the light of the nations. This Christocentric theology would come to shape much of the council's work.

In the original text as submitted by Cardinal Ottaviani, when speaking of the requirement on obedience, members of the church were referred to as **"subjects,"** much as a king might refer to the subjects who live within his realm. In this revision, that language was utterly gone and replaced instead with an understanding that members of the church form the **people of God**.[26]

Perhaps the most significant change from that first version of this schema was the inclusion of chapter four. In this chapter, the authors of the revised schema teach that **Jesus calls everyone to holiness**. Holiness is not reserved only for the ordained or consecrated religious, but also for each and every baptized person. Such holiness is lived in everyday life as people respond to their neighbors with love, the document taught. It should be noted that this idea faced no resistance in the council and soon became a leitmotif of nearly every document.

October 4–28, 1963 ▶ The debate on chapter two of **the revised schema on the church** continued with a discussion of collegiality that lasted for ten days. Also among other debated points were the following: (1) whether to include a chapter on Mary in the document on the church or to have a separate document devoted to her; (2) the nature of the church; (3) the role and place of the laity; (4) the reinstitution of a permanent and possibly married diaconate; (5) ecumenical questions; (6) the relationship of church and state; (7) the universal call to holiness; (8) religious orders; and others.

The overall discussion on this document lasted **for 23 days** and was characterized by rather long, somewhat dull, and repetitious, speeches. But even after this long debate, no final document was in sight because, according to the procedures, any revisions would have to come from the Theological Commission, headed by Cardinal Ottaviani. He was intentionally working at a plodding pace, only convening the commission once each week, and sometimes less often. It gradually became clear that the pace of revision would be plodding, which was a great frustration for the council fathers.

Clearly, Cardinal Ottaviani didn't consider speeches on the council floor to have any legislative force. It was equally clear that any outcomes might take several years to be finalized, dashing the hopes of those who wanted to reform more quickly. **A crisis was underway in the council** as these sentiments of despair took hold among the bishops.

October 22, 1963 ▶ Cardinal Suenens urged that the number of lay people present at the council be increased and that **the number should include women.** "Unless I am mistaken," he said, "women make up one half of the world's population."

October 23, 1963 ▶ **A summit meeting of council leaders** was held to try to move the stalled council, but little progress was reported. The next day, it was announced that the following Monday, October 28, no general congregation of the council would be held. Instead, Pope Paul would preside at a special Mass in memory of Pope John. Cardinal Suenens would give the address. On the Sunday evening before this, Cardinal Suenens and Pope Paul dined privately together. Meanwhile, the debate—and the standoff between Cardinal Ottaviani and the bishops who favored more reform—continued.

October 24, 1963 ▶ Dr. Edmund Schlink of the University of Heidelberg and the Evangelical Lutheran Church of Germany spoke on behalf of most of the separated and Orthodox Christians in saying that **even the revised schema on the church** was defective because it gave no recognition to churches that were not in communion with Rome. "It appears," he says, "more Roman than catholic."

October 28, 1963 ▶ The 8:30 AM Mass was celebrated as planned with Pope Paul presiding. After Mass, **Cardinal Suenens approached the pulpit,** appearing calm and serious. He carefully took out his glasses and put them on. He unfolded his notes, paused, and looked at Pope Paul who was seated on his throne. Then he began his speech. He spoke in French—a significant departure from the Latin of the council. He had also distributed copies of his text in other languages to be sure he was heard and understood by all. Although he did not mention "the crisis" explicitly (that is, the continual stalling of progress by the slow work of the Doctrinal Commission and its challenge to the legitimacy of the vote late in the previous period), his speech was clearly an attempt to move the council forward—and it was clear as well that he was speaking for the pope. He recalled the memory of John XXIII, quoting his very words: "We have no reason to be afraid. Fear comes only from a lack of faith." He ended by calling the council to its task of making the gospel understandable in today's world. Long applause greeted his speech. He left the pulpit and approached the throne of the pope, who was smiling broadly. He bent and kissed his ring. Then the pope rose and embraced him, embracing as well his words. A second round of applause filled the basilica.

October 30, 1963 ▶ Cardinal Suenens, still frustrated by the lack of progress and the continued stalling tactics of the Roman Curia, had (on October 15) offered the council **five proposals,** asking for a vote to determine the mind of the council on the place of bishops in the church. The members of the curia and the more cautious bishops who feared reform considered this "illegal" because the proposals had not come from them. On **October 30, a vote was taken.** The overwhelming outcome supported Cardinal Suenens and the position of the large group of world's bishops who favored more reform.

October 29 to November 7, 1962 ▶ The debate on **the revised schema on the church** continued amid claims from Cardinal Ottaviani that the vote was not binding. This was the vote which had occurred on October 30 and which showed overwhelming support for the point of view of the pope and the bishops who favored more reform. Furthermore, open accusations were made that the schema was being altered in ways not approved by the assembly. Public calls were made to reduce the prominence of the members of the curia.

Despite the intervention of Suenens and the pope, the stagnation and crisis continued. The attacks grew more biting and more and more personal in nature. There was a growing feeling that the church's administrators in the curia were acting like legislators, a role belonging solely to the bishops. They were indeed trying to undermine the council by refusing to move forward.

November 8, 1963 ▶ In response to this crisis, **Cardinal Frings of Cologne** spoke in favor of the reform of the Roman Curia, saying that the members of the curia must not confuse administrative roles with legislative ones. The methods and behavior of the members of the curia, he said, did not conform at all to the modern era and were a cause of scandal to the world. He was referring mainly to the judgmental approach of the Holy Office, headed by Cardinal Ottaviani, and to their secret proceedings against many theologians. His remarks were met with loud and prolonged applause, even though that was forbidden in the debates. It should be noted that for many bishops, the applause of recent weeks was their only way to find the full expression of their shared point of view.

Shaking with anger and emotion, **Cardinal Ottaviani responded** that in criticizing the Holy Office, one attacks the pope himself. He went on to claim that his commission is the only group that can define collegiality. His remarks, too, were met with applause, but it was light in comparison with the response of the majority. This exchange brought the debate into the open and was clearly the most dramatic discussion of the council to this date as the "new order" of collegiality of bishops was juxtaposed with the "old order."

On the same day ▶ In another unrelated but essential matter, a communiqué was issued regarding **the attitude of Catholics toward non-Christians,** especially the Jews. The paper stated clearly that the Jews were not guilty of the death of Jesus and called for respect and mutual understanding.

November 18, 1963 ▶ **The schema on ecumenism** was introduced for debate. The document was primarily hailed as both sound in doctrine and pastorally oriented. It generated great enthusiasm on the floor of the council, in part because of Cardinal Bea's tireless efforts as head of the Secretariat for Christian Unity. Cardinal Bea's report on the matter was listened to reverently and greeted with an ovation. At one point, Cardinal Leger of Canada said, "The present hope for and movement toward unity are not passing impulses, but are inspired by the Gospel and the Holy Spirit."

Background

Only a small number of more cautious bishops who feared reform opposed the schema. One of them, Cardinal Ruffini, spoke at the November 29 debate, expressing the view of that group that the Roman Catholic Church has nothing to learn and nothing to be sorry for. "We strongly hope," he says, "that our separated brethren will again embrace the Catholic Church of Rome." Dialogue, he says, has only one purpose: to "bring back" those in error to the real church. In the end, it became clear that this was a point of view held by only a small group of bishops but not by most of the bishops of the world.

Initially, a draft document on religious liberty was included in the schema on ecumenism and reported to the council by Bishop De Smedt of Belgium. Religious liberty was defined as "the right to free exercise of religion according to the dictates of conscience. Looked at negatively," the report goes on, "it means immunity from outside coercion." Eventually, the question of religious liberty was framed in a declaration of its own and promulgated near the end of the final period of the council.

November 21, 1963 ▶ Again, in response to the crisis, Pope Paul **enlarged the commissions** intending to expedite their work and forestall the delaying tactics of the more cautious bishops who feared reform.

November 22, 1963 ▶ **The document providing for the sweeping reform of the liturgy** was approved at 12:05 PM by the council fathers. The vote to send this document to Pope Paul for promulgation was an overwhelming 2,159 to 19. Prolonged applause greeted the announcement of the vote.

On the same day ▶ **President John Kennedy was assassinated** in the United States at about 7:00 PM Roman time, sending a hush upon the whole city of Rome. One news commentator wrote that in a single year, two great Catholic men named John—Pope John XXIII and President John Kennedy—died, having initiated much work which they left unfinished.

November 25, 1963 ▶ **The document on communications media** was approved by the council fathers by a vote of 1,598 to 503. The unusually sizeable negative vote resulted from a widespread sense in the council that, while this matter might merit some attention, it was not worthy of the actions of a council. This document was seen as out of step with other council outcomes, somewhat condescending in tone, and reflecting a view of the press that was unrealistic. It may have been that Pope Paul allowed the document to pass as it did to move it off the council's agenda so they could get on to more meaningful work.

December 1, 1963 ▶ Cardinal Bea graciously summed up the council **debate on ecumenism** and promised to give the recommendations of the council fathers careful consideration in revising the schema for the third session.

December 3, 1963 ▶ **A petition,** signed by 200 council fathers from 46 nations, asking for a particular schema to condemn Communism, Marxism, and Socialism, was presented to the papal secretary of state. No such schema ever reached the council floor, and the only condemnation issued by this council related to the nuclear arms race and notion of deterrence.

On the same day ▶ **Two laymen addressed the council** to support the movement toward ecumenism and the expanding role of lay people in the church. They were Jean Guitton of France and Vittonino Veronese of Italy.

December 4, 1963 ▶ **The second period of the Second Vatican Council closed** with a solemn liturgy and the promulgation of the first two documents from the council. The final, official voting was decisive:
- **The Constitution on the Sacred Liturgy:**
    2,147 to 4
- **The Decree on Communications:**
    1,960 to 164

There was a general sense among the council fathers that progress in this second period had been slow, as it had been in the first period. Pope Paul also took this occasion to announce his plan to visit the Holy Land between periods. The third annual period was set to begin on September 14, 1964.

The Interim Period Between Annual Periods 2 and 3

December 1963 to September 1964

January 1964 ▶ **Pope Paul VI** (who is the bishop of Rome) **and Patriarch Athenagoras I** (who is the bishop of Constantinople) met in a historic gesture of reconciliation in the Holy Land while both were on pilgrimage there. They met three times. The first meeting was at the pope's place of residence in the Holy Land, where he greeted the patriarch with the gift of a chalice and said that he hopes they will one day share it again. The second meeting was at the patriarch's place of residence in the Holy Land, where he greeted the pope with the gift of a pectoral chain, symbolic of a bishop's apostolic succession; Pope Paul immediately donned the pectoral chain. The third meeting was an accidental one on the street where they stood for ten minutes of intimate visiting.

This carefully planned meeting, the first between the pope and the patriarch since the Middle Ages, resulted in a significant move forward in relations between the Churches of the East and the West. It laid the groundwork for work still to be done on the document on ecumenism, which was on the agenda for the third period of the council.

September 13, 1964 ▶ On the day before the third period of the council was set to open, **Pope Paul received a letter signed by some 25 cardinals** among others, all from that more cautious group of bishops who feared reform, warning against the dangers of moving forward with greater collegiality in the church. This letter was part of a more extensive campaign by those who feared any challenge to the primacy and authority of the pope, and collegiately seemed to them like such a challenge. In the end, this campaign was mostly successful.

The letter outlined what this group wanted, which was that the pope should intervene and suspend the council. They asked that he appoint a commission on the matter of collegiality and return to the council at some future date. Pope Paul was not happy with this and he let it be known. In response, he consulted Archbishop

Pericle Felici (Secretary of the Council) who advised the pope in these words: "In the end, it is necessary to have faith in the consciences of the council fathers, in the force of truth, and above all, in the help of the Holy Spirit." Pope Paul immediately dropped the idea of postponement—but the matter did not end there.

The Third Annual Period
September to November 1964

September 14, 1964 ▶ **The third annual period opened** with a concelebrated mass in St. Peter's. It should be noted that concelebration had only been restored to the church with the Constitution on the Liturgy promulgated at the end of the previous period of the council. Before this, all Masses in the council were presided by one bishop while all the others said "private Masses" in the chapels of their various residences around Rome.

Pope Paul's opening remarks were a call to the council fathers **to define the place of the bishop in the church**, an effort which had thus far proved to be frustrating for the council fathers because of the tactics of the curia to prevent this idea moving forward. These latter saw it as a challenge to their ecclesiastical powers.

September 15, 1964 ▶ **New rules** were announced, which were generally seen to benefit the smaller group of more cautious bishops and the members of the curia. In general, they were designed (1) to limit the activity of theological experts, known as *periti*, who were working with the bishops and (2) to prevent the distribution of "unauthorized" documents such as position papers, the observations of theologians regarding specific questions, and so forth. Most of these papers were, of course, written and distributed in the vernacular and often translated into a variety of modern languages.

September 16, 1964 ▶ A vote was taken on chapter one of **the revised schema on the church.** The chapter was overwhelmingly approved: 2,189 to 11. (63 of the yes votes were cast with reservations attached.) This first chapter provided the essential principles about the nature of the church on which the rest of the document would rest. The chapter was entitled, "The Mystery of the Church" and said, among other things, that the church is a mystery or a sacrament of Jesus, who is the Christ. It is imbued with the hidden presence of God.

September 18, 1964 ▶ Four votes were taken on various articles composing chapter 2 of **the revised schema on the church:** the voting again ran overwhelmingly in favor of this chapter, averaging 2,128 in support and 39 opposed. This chapter defined the church as the people of God.

It should be noted that this revised schema, composed principally by Monsignor Gerard Philips of the Diocese of Liege in Belgium, replaced the schema introduced by Cardinal Ottaviani. It could not have been easy for the cardinal to see such widespread support for a schema which he felt was inadequate and may even have regarded as invalid since it did not emerge from his Doctrinal Commission first.

September 21, 1964 ▶ Voting began on various parts of chapter 3 of **the revised schema on the church**—the chapter on bishops and their collegiality—and continued through eight council workdays. The voting was overwhelmingly in favor of collegiality, with only a small minority continuing to oppose the concept. This chapter, as Pope Paul pointed out in his opening address for the third period, formed the core work of this council. Vatican I had defined only the primacy of the papacy and the doctrine of infallibility. The work on collegiality being done in Vatican II, in a sense, would complete the unfinished work of Vatican I.

The anti-collegiality group, however, saw this move as dangerous because they feared it would weaken the role of the curia, which they believed was solely capable of governing the church. On September 21, as the voting began, Archbishop Pietro Parente, thought to be opposed to it, announced his support for the notion of collegiality, urging the council fathers not to fear that a breakdown of the church would result. The smaller, more cautious anti-collegiality group was predicting precisely such a collapse. His support proved to be a fatal blow to the hope of the resistance.

September 23, 1964 ▶ The debate on **the declaration on religious liberty** was opened. Father John Courtney Murray SJ, an American *peritus*, was mostly responsible for this document, which most of the bishops at the council, including those from the United States, strongly supported.

On the same day ▶ **Eight women religious and seven lay unmarried women** were named as auditors at the council. In his opening speech for this session, the pope had said, "And we are delighted to welcome among the auditors our beloved daughters in Christ, the first women in history to participate in a conciliar assembly."

Background

The women included:

- Mother Savine de Valon—superior general of the Religious of the Sacred Heart and president of the Union of Superiors General
- Mother Mary Luke Tobin—superior general of the Sisters of Loreto in Kentucky, USA, and president of the Conference of Major Religious Superiors of Women's Institutes of America
- Mother Marie de la Croix Khouzan—superior general of the Egyptian Sisters of the Sacred Heart and president of the Union of Teaching Religious in Egypt
- Mother Marie Henritee Ghanem— superior general of the Sisters of the Sacred Hearts of Jesus and Mary and president of the Assembly of Major Religious Superiors in Lebanon
- Sister Mary Juliana of our Lord Jesus Christ—secretary general of the Union of Major Religious Superiors in Germany
- Mother Guillemin—superior general of the Daughters of Charity
- Mother Estrada—superior general of the Servants of the Sacred Heart in Spain
- Mother Baldinucci—superior general of the Institute of the Most Holy Child Mary in Italy

- Dr. Alda Micelli—president-general of the Missionaries of the Kingdom of Christ
- Miss Pilar Belosiool—president of the World Union of Catholic Women's Organizations in Spain
- Miss Rosemary Goldie—executive secretary of the Permanent Committee for International Congresses of the Lay Apostolate in Australia
- Miss Marie Louise Monnet—president of the international movement for the apostolate in independent social circles in France
- Miss Anna Maria Roeloffzen—secretary of the International Federation of Feminine Catholic Youth in the Netherlands
- Marchioness Amalia Lanza—a war widow

- Ms. Idducia Marenco—a war widow

September 28, 1964 ▶ The declaration on the Jews (whose Latin name was eventually *Nostra Aetate*) was presented for debate in the council. The debate produced a statement more inclusive of Muslims and other non-Christians in addition to a more strongly worded and clearly stated passage ending the notion that the Jews are somehow guilty for the death of Jesus, a charge known as "deicide." It should be noted that the term *deicide*, which refers to the idea that the Jews had killed Jesus, was the basis of most persecution of the Jews throughout the centuries.

September 30, 1964 ▶ The revised schema on divine revelation was presented for debate. Most of the council fathers favored its approach to Scripture. They saw it as consistent with the modern biblical movement, including the encyclicals of Pope Pius XII on the matter: *Divino Afflante Spiritu* in 1943 and *Humani Generis* in 1951.

October 6, 1964 ▶ The schema on the lay apostolate was presented for debate. Most council fathers saw it as clerical in tone, as though the role of the laity was to "assist" the clergy, using the Catholic Action Movement as its basis. It should be noted that the 1917 code of canon law had defined a layperson merely as "one who is not a cleric."

It was also seen as lacking a solid theological basis in the sacrament of baptism. Furthermore, although the document dealt with the laity, no laity had been consulted on it until the last minute. Bishop Alexander Carter of the Diocese of Sault Sainte Marie, Ontario Canada, said that the document was "conceived in the sin of clericalism." Archbishop D'Souza of Bhopal India said that it's high time to treat the laity like "grownups. Laymen (sic) must be treated as brothers (sic) by the clergy," he said.

October 9, 1964 ▶ Cardinal Suenens called for **a broader definition of the role of the laity** in the church before continuing the debate on the document dealing with them.

October 12, 1964 ▶ A so-called "October Crisis" threatened the council. In an effort to bury the schemas on the Jews and on religious liberty, the more cautious bishops who feared reform and many of the members of the curia—through the pen of Cardinal Felici—attempted to derail the progress of the two documents. Felici sent a letter to Cardinal Bea, head of the Secretariat responsible for their preparation, requiring that he submit these documents to the conservatively oriented Theological Commission for revision. In his letter, Felici suggested he was speaking for the pope. Despite the well-known efforts of this small group of more cautious bishops to control the outcome of the council, **this bold demand stunned everyone**. The leaders of the bishops favoring more reform met to respond. In firm and concise language, they drafted an appeal to the pope, asking him for clarification. The pope, in turn, assured them that these two documents would indeed remain under Cardinal Bea's jurisdiction, but he struck a compromise by allowing the Theological Commission to "examine" the documents.

When the letter to the pope from those in favor of the document was released, the whole affair **boiled over into the press**—and the official Vatican newspaper heavily criticized the press for publishing it. Clearly, the modern church had lessons to learn about the ways of the news media as well as those of Christian charity to do its work.

It should be noted that the letter to the pope asking for clarification began with the Latin words *magno cum dolore*— "with great sorrow"—which historians have said characterized the entire third session due to the wrangling of the tenacious and wily conservative minority.

October 13, 1964 ▶ The debate began on **the schema dealing with priestly life and ministry**. The document, which had been distributed the year before, had now been reduced to a series of propositions. This was seen as insufficient by most in the council. Cardinal Meyer of Chicago spoke for many when he pointed out that the council had thoroughly debated the place of bishops and the place of the laity in the modern church. There should also be, he said, a full debate on the position of priests lest the outcome be a medieval model of the priesthood in an otherwise modern church. On October 19, an overwhelming majority sent the document back to its commission for revision.

October 15, 1964 ▶ **The schema on Eastern Catholic Churches** (those in union with Rome) was introduced for debate. In general, the schema was seen as insufficient in dealing with the place of the patriarchs and was thought by many an attempt to "Romanize" the East. Eastern Rite prelates were the most vociferous in their criticism. It should be noted that all of these Eastern Churches are in union with Rome and were in the hall throughout the council.

October 20, 1964 ▶ The document dealing with **the church in the modern world**, known in the council as **Schema 13** and long-awaited by all, was introduced for debate. This document had been called for in the first period by Cardinals Suenens and Montini in their response to the first version of the schema on the church (submitted by Cardinal Ottaviani but rejected by the assembly). On the first day of debate, eight cardinals spoke on Schema 13. Seven spoke of it favorably, and the council adopted it as the basis for their debate, something they had not done with many other documents.

October 22, 1964 ▶ Archbishop John Heenan of West-minster, England, **spoke strongly against Schema 13,** saying he considered it "dangerous." It is the work of the *periti,* he said, not the council fathers themselves. His remarks, because of their vehemence, stunned most of the bishops.

October 23, 1964 ▶ Bishop Guano of Livorno, Italy, announced to the assembled fathers that **the pope had reserved to himself the decisions on birth control** because a commission had been established to study the matter the previous June. He said the pope does not feel it wise to anticipate the results of that group's work. This disappointed many bishops from poor nations who had hoped for an update in church teaching desperately needed in their countries. In the end, as is well known, the so-called "birth control commission" voted 56-4 in favor of allowing certain modern means of regulating conception. Pope Paul VI, concerned that a change in teaching on this matter would weaken church teaching on other issues, eventually published in 1966 **the encyclical, *Humane Vitae.*** Siding with the minority of four, it re-affirmed the church's teaching regarding married love and the rejection of artificial contraception.

October 26, 1964 ▶ Bishop Louis Morrow, a Texas-born bishop

serving in Krishnagar, India, said that he was speaking in the name of millions who did not understand **the church's teaching on hell**. There is, he says, a **"lack of proportion"** between the sin of eating meat on Friday and the eternal hellfire, which is the punishment for such a sin. The current teaching, he went on to say, puts one who eats meat on Friday in the same category as an atheist or an adulterer. In order for the church to be believable, he argued, more balance must become part of our teaching on this and other matters.

October 29–30, 1964 ▶ The discussion on the section on **marriage and birth control in the schema on The Church in the Modern World** got underway. Despite the announcement on October 23, just a few days earlier, that Pope Paul had reserved this decision to himself, many spoke on the matter. Cardinal Dearden of Detroit, Michigan in the United States presented marriage as ordered toward God, the love of the couple, and the procreation of children, in that order.

Background

Cardinal Leger of Montreal in Canada challenged the status quo by saying that "the intimate union of the spouses also finds a purpose in love. And this end is truly the end of the act (i.e., of intercourse) itself, even when it is not ordained to procreation."

Cardinal Suenens of Mechelen-Brussels in Belgium called for a council commission to work with the papal group studying birth control to ensure that the church's teaching will be in keeping with modern times. "I beg of you, my brother bishops," he says, "let us avoid a new **'Galileo affair.'** One is enough for the church."

Maximos IV Saigh was Patriarch of Antioch and All the East, and Alexandria and Jerusalem of the Melkite Greek Catholic Church from 1947 until his death in 1967. At 87-years-old, his words had often called the council to realism in previous debates. He said now that this is an "urgent problem because it lies at the root of a great crisis of the Catholic conscience. The faithful," he said, "find themselves **forced to live in conflict with the law of the church**, far from the sacraments in constant anguish, unable to find a viable solution between two contradictory imperatives: conscience and normal married life. Frankly," he went on to say, "can the official positions of the church in this matter not be reviewed in the light of modern theological, medical, psychological, and sociological science?" He continued, "and are we not entitled to ask if certain positions are not the outcome of outmoded ideas and, perhaps, *a bachelor psychosis* on the part of those unacquainted with this sector of life?" (italics are mine).[27]

On the other side of the debate, Cardinal Ottaviani of the curia said, "I am not pleased with the statement of the text that married couples can determine the number of children they are to have. This has never been heard of before in the church."

Cardinal Browne, the Titular Archbishop of Idebessus (an ancient city in modern Turkey, solely a title held by the cardinal), an Irish Dominican who served as Master General of his order until made a cardinal in 1962, repeated the scholastic doctrine: "The primary end of marriage," he said, "is procreation and the education of children. The secondary end is, on the one hand, the mutual aid of the spouses, and on the other, a remedy for concupiscence (i.e., sexual desire)."

Shortly after that, the debate abruptly ended. Two days later, Cardinal Alfredo Ottaviani, in a worldwide news conference, said that the church's teaching on this matter would never change because that teaching is based "on the natural law and several scriptural texts."

Before the debate on Schema 13 ended, the council fathers dealt with sections on **atheism, the church and the world, racial discrimination, culture, economic and social life, and nuclear war.**

November 6, 1964 ▶ The discussion on Schema 13 was interrupted so the **pope could visit the council.** Under pressure from some advisers, he introduced **the schema on missionary activity** and called for its passage. This document, however, had been poorly drawn together and needed a great deal more work. The council fathers promptly sent the document back to the commission which drafted it, an embarrassment for the pope.

November 10, 1964 ▶ The schema on **the renewal of religious life** was introduced for debate. The large group of bishops who favored reform desired a more comprehensive view for this document—and a more thorough renewal of religious life than the first draft provided for. This was true especially in cases where a rigorous monastic regime competed with a heavy pastoral workload, causing many men and women religious to leave their communities. Two days later, the council fathers sent the document back to its commission for revision.

November 12, 1964 ▶ The schema on **priestly formation** was introduced for debate. The draft was generally found acceptable to most, a rare occurrence at the council. The document called for seminary programs more in keeping with the times, ones that develop the personalities and psychological health as well as the intellects of seminarians.

November 17, 1964 ▶ The schema on **Christian education** was introduced for debate. The council fathers found it generally acceptable and added only minor changes.

November 19, 1964 ▶ *Lumen Gentium*, **the Constitution on the Church,** was passed, 2,134 to 10 but not until Pope Paul had attached to it what would be known as the *Nota Praevia*. On November 16, Archbishop Felici distributed this *Nota Praevia*, which was attached to chapter three of this Constitution. The note had come from the pope himself. As Felici put it, the note came "from a higher authority." This launched what would come to be known as "the worst week of Vatican II." It caused anger, confusion, and frustration among the vast majority of council fathers who favored reform.

On the other hand, this move on the part of the pope greatly pleased the cautious group of bishops who feared reform. Many of the latter group now felt free to vote in favor of *Lumen Gentium* and they did so on this day, November 19. This almost certainly was Pope Paul's goal.

Background

What to do with this *Nota*? Such a note had never before been used in the history of the church. Was it simply meant to clarify? Or was it now, in fact, part of the official document? The *nota* had been authored by Gerard Philips (who also authored the revised schema that was now under consideration as the Constitution on the Church). He argued that it did not change the meaning of the text. But Joseph Ratzinger, serving as a *peritus* or theological consultant to Cardinal Frings of Cologne, Germany, saw it tipping the balance in favor of the primacy of the pope.[28]

In any case, the Constitution on the Church passed by a wide margin.

November 19, 1964 ▶ A discussion on the **sacrament of marriage** was held, and a document calling for a renewal in canon law governing matrimony was sent to the pope to be included in a future post-conciliar decree.

On this same day ▶ Cardinal Tisserant, president for the day, announced that **no vote would be taken in this session of the council on the schema on religious liberty**. The members of the curia had taken advantage of a minor rule to manipulate this postponement in order, they hoped, to kill the document. Immediately, petitions were circulated on the floor of the council, and nearly 1,000 signers called on the pope to intervene to stop this move.

In the end, however, the pope allowed the smaller group of more cautious bishops to sway him, causing anger, resentment, and hostility. November 19, 1964, became known as **Black Thursday** in council history because of these actions on the part of this small, cautious group of bishops and the pope's failure to counteract them. The pope did promise, however, that this schema would be treated first in the fourth (and next) annual period.

On this same day ▶ There was also a move by the same small group of cautious bishops to postpone action on the schema on **Ecumenism.** To please the members of the curia, Pope Paul sent last-minute changes to this document. Cardinal Bea would have to write them into the document before the council could vote on it. Not as strong as the *Nota Praevia*, this was nonetheless an indication that Pope Paul's "red pencil" was at work again.

There was a general sense in the council that **time was running out** because this was to have been its third and final session. Much work remained to be done, however, on multiple schemas, including the critical and controversial schema 13, on **The Church in the Modern World.** The small cautious group of bishops who had won the ear of Pope Paul had been successful in delaying final action on several items—a sense of gloom was palpable in these final days.

November 20, 1964 ▶ A large majority approved the **Declaration** on **The Church's Relations with non-Christians** (*Nostra Aetate*).

The **Decree on Eastern Catholic Churches** was also approved for promulgation the following day.

Likewise, the **Decree on Ecumenism** was approved, including 19 out of the 40 last-minute changes ordered by the pope.

November 21, 1964 ▶ **The third period was closed** by Pope Paul VI who took the occasion—which was a surprise to almost everyone—to **proclaim Mary the Mother of the church,** a move which greatly disappointed the Protestant observers, confused most bishops, and added to the generally gloomy feeling at the end of this stormy session. Why would the Pope take it on himself to do this? What message was he sending about his commitment to the council? Under whose influence did he act? The council fathers, in a carefully worked out agreement, had included a chapter on Mary in the Constitution on the Church, so why would Pope Paul do this and why now?

Three documents were promulgated on this final day of the third period, bringing the total for the first three periods to five. The voting on the documents was decisive:
- **The Constitution on the Church:**
  2,151 to 5
- **The Decree on Ecumenism:**
  2,137 to 11
- **The Decree on Eastern Churches:**
  2,110 to 39

The Interim Period Between Annual Periods 3 and 4

November 1964 to September 1965

December 2-5, 1964 ▶ Pope Paul VI attended the worldwide **Eucharistic Congress in India,** a trip hailed as successful by most.

January 1965 ▶ Pope Paul VI ordered that **a letter be sent to the heads of curial offices** in the Vatican, reminding them that they have come under heavy criticism, including his own, and that they are to be "docile" as reforms of the curia itself are announced, presumably soon. There was a growing attitude on the part of the members of the curia and that small group of cautious bishops—who formed a minority in the council—that the bishops of the world could not be trusted with the scope of the reform they had undertaken at Vatican II thus far. These members of the curia believed that they alone possessed the insight and faith needed to govern the church, and they feared any further move toward collegiality would diminish their power to do so.

February 19, 1965 ▶ Cardinal Bea visited the **World Council of Churches** international center in Geneva and shared the dais with its president, Pastor Marc Boegner of France, in the Hall of the Reformation. In a historic exchange, both expressed the hope that cooperation "based on love" would lead to closer unity.

Background

During this interim period, it became apparent to those working on the commissions that fully reformed, biblically-based, uniformly open documents on the matters before the council would not be possible. **Compromise and negotiation would be necessary** if the council was to reach a successful end.

It also became clear during this period that the sluggish pace of the first three sessions was due mainly to **the tactics of the members of the curia and a small but vocal and cautious group of cardinals and bishops.** This was demonstrated boldly in their delay of the schemas on ecumenism and religious liberty, for example.

The schema on religious liberty did come to a vote early in the fourth period, as promised by Pope Paul. It passed 1,997 to 224, showing how small the minority really was. But it was also clear that **Pope Paul had not acted decisively to counter this minority's tactics**. These curial insiders, after all, had daily access to the pope, especially Cardinals Cicognani (secretary of state in the Vatican) and Felici (secretary-general of the council). Why did the pope not trust the bishops of the world who had expressed their sentiments so clearly in the council? Why did he bend to the wishes of these insiders whom he wished to reform, rather than the majority of the college of cardinals and bishops?

Judgments are never fair, but certain Vatican observers and some members of the press found Pope Paul worrisome and timid, overly committed to gradualism, unwilling to anger the curia by acting against its desire for the status quo, and unable or unwilling to make decisions in the face of conflicting advice. On the other hand, Pope Paul may very well have been acting under the influence of the Holy Spirit in his desire for great unanimity among council fathers, and maybe his interventions in the third period were aimed at securing that and avoiding schism.

March 7, 1965 ▶ Showing his support for the reform of the liturgy, Pope Paul began **celebrating Mass in the vernacular** on the very first day it was permitted.

June 10, 1965 ▶ Pope Paul VI **"rehabilitated"** Galileo Galilei. In the early seventeenth century, this Italian astronomer had been humiliated by the church, which in 1633 forced him to kneel before the Holy Inquisition and recant his Copernican belief that the sun—not the earth—was the center of the universe. Galileo was then placed under house arrest until his death four years later. It should be noted that this rehabilitation by Pope Paul VI does not actually admit error on the part of the church or the medieval popes involved with Galileo's silencing.

August 4, 1965 ▶ During this and other summer general audiences, **Pope Paul spoke of the anxieties** he felt as the fourth session approached. He spoke of the many issues facing the church and the "burden they place upon us." Confirming the judgment of observers mentioned above, he repeatedly referred to the fear he has of anything other than very gradual reform. Further evidence of this fear is seen in his failure to enact any meaningful reform in the curia, despite his repeated calls for this reform.

September 12, 1965 ▶ The weekend before the opening of the fourth period, **Pope Paul issued his third encyclical,** *Mysterium Fidei,* in which he insinuated that the Catholic faith is threatened by certain nameless quarters where debate and dialogue are taking place. This was seen as a reprimand to the Dutch, Belgian, and French theological circles where a discussion on the nature of the Eucharist was underway.

The Fourth Annual Period
September to December 1965

September 14, 1965 ▶ **The fourth annual period of Vatican II opened.** Pope Paul presided at a simple ceremony, lacking the pomp of previous openings. In the homily, he avoided discussion of the issues before the council and called only for charity in dealing with one another. He also announced his intention to visit the United Nations in the fall. In what seemed at the time to be the best news of all, he announced his intention to establish a synod of bishops to advise him. It should be noted that the formation of such a group had been called for since the beginning of the council and was part of the movement toward collegiality among bishops.

September 15, 1965 ▶ **Pope Paul attended the first general congregation** (or working meeting) of the fourth period. While there, the *motu proprio* entitled *Apostolica Sollicitudo* was read aloud, actually establishing the synod of bishops promised only the day before. No one had expected such rapid action. However, this move on the part of Pope Paul was not quite as positive as it might have seemed. In establishing the synod, he made it clear that it was subject to the immediate and direct power of the pope. It was a synod but one without authority of any kind except what the pope yielded to it, which seemed to be very little. He never used the word collegiality in the *motu proprio* so that in the end, it was more a statement of papal prerogative than of anything else.

On the same day ▶ The schema on **religious liberty,** as promised, was reintroduced for discussion. The scope of the document, as made clear by Bishop de Smedt of the Diocese of Bruges in Belgium, was to address the question of "the human and civil right to liberty in religious matters." That is, it would address the extent to which individuals or groups should be free from coercion in matters of religion. The document defended the place of conscience in such matters, as well as the notion that doctrine develops over time. Both of these latter matters raised concerns among the small but cautious group of bishops who did not support this document.

It should be noted that a significant statement on conscience was also included in the Constitution on the Church in the Modern World, article sixteen.

Background

Most of the bishops generally favored the revised document (on religious liberty), citing the growing worldwide movement toward personal independence and civil liberty, separating civil from religious institutions. **A smaller, more cautious group of bishops** were against separating state and church. One Spanish cardinal said that only the Catholic Church has the right to preach the gospel. Therefore, he argued, others who want to seek converts in Catholic countries must be suppressed, even by the state. Cardinal Ottaviani declared that only the Catholic Church has a legitimate, natural, and objective right to liberty. This attitude—held only by that small group of cautious bishops but not by most of the bishops of the world—is in direct contradiction to the spirit of the document on religious liberty.

Some who oppose the document on religious liberty feared it would compromise the claim of the Catholic Church to be "the one true church," while others feared the idea of basing a person's right to religious freedom on the dignity of the human person. In general, American prelates, coming from their long tradition of religious tolerance in the United States, jubilantly hailed the document. (An American, John Courtney Murray SJ, had drafted the document.) Bishops from heavily Catholic countries tended to oppose it, along with the small and cautious group of bishops, many of whom were also members of the curia. Bishops from countries where the church was undergoing persecution (Communist and Socialist mainly) strongly favored it, including Cardinal Wojtyla of Krakow, who was eventually chosen as Pope John Paul II.

Despite the many speeches in favor, it seemed that this declaration (on religious liberty) was running into trouble and might not come to a general vote in the council at all.

September 21, 1965 ▶ Pope Paul summoned certain council leaders to his apartment in the Vatican and ordered that a vote on **religious liberty** be taken at once. (The previous evening, a decision by the council's leadership had decided against taking such a general vote.) Immediately, the secretary-general, Cardinal Felici, announced that a vote would be taken. The results were **a landslide for the large group of bishops from around the world who favored reform:** 1,997 in favor, 224 opposed.

With that behind them, the council fathers turn their attention back to the schema on **The Church in the Modern World (Schema 13).** This unique document, the first-ever directed by a council to "all humankind," had been drafted in French because modern thought can be expressed understandably only in a contemporary language. It was also the only conciliar document made available in other modern languages, rather than in Latin. At this point, it was in its fourth revision and was massive, running 80 pages in length!

The mood of the council as the discussion on Schema 13 got underway was much more optimistic than at the end of the third session, owing in large part to the establishment of the synod of bishops and the overwhelmingly positive vote on religious liberty.

September 27, 1965 ▶ The debate on **The Church in the Modern World** saw repeated calls for a strongly worded section condemning atheism, especially Marxist atheism. The schema was seen as overly optimistic, very western in tone, and put together somewhat hastily. Nonetheless, it gradually gained support throughout the short debate which lasted only three weeks.

September 29, 1965 ▶ The debate on **The Church in the Modern World** turned its attention to **marriage** once again. Many felt that this section of the document lacked sufficient strength because the pope was reserving to himself the decision about the place of birth control in modern Catholic life, considered by most council fathers as the huge issue of married life in that day. It was generally felt that the document did not give adequate prominence to the vital place of sexual intercourse in the lives of married couples.

Fr. Edward Schillebeeckx, a Dutch Dominican sacramental scholar steeped in the *ressourcement* employed at the council, taught at the Catholic University in Nijmegen. He gave a well-attended conference on the changing nature of Christian marriage in the modern world.

September 30, 1965 ▶ The long-awaited revised schema on *Nostra Aetate*, the declaration which addressed the church's relationship with non-Christians, especially the Jews, was released. It quickly became known, however, that the members of the Roman Curia who prepared the document omitted **the term** *deicide* even though more than 90 percent of the council fathers had ordered its reinsertion at an earlier meeting of the council. The council fathers wanted a clear statement that the Jews are not guilty of "God-killing" and never were. However, for those bishops living in Arab states on the eastern end of the Mediterranean, the question was not quite as simple because of secular political considerations in their home dioceses. There had been public demonstrations against this document in some cities in this area. In the end, Pope Paul once again helped find a middle road that prevented division in the council while still providing a strong statement on non-Christian religions of many kinds, including the Jews. In the end, the declaration was promulgated without the term deicide in it.

October 1, 1965 ▶ Voting on the decree concerned with the pastoral duties of **bishops** was concluded and received overwhelming approval. Almost immediately, the U.S. bishops named a commission to establish formal contact with the **American Jewish community.**

October 4, 1965 ▶ Two events coincided. First, **Pope Paul VI traveled to the United Nations** in New York City, where he delivered an address, the first-ever by a pope, calling on the nations of the world to cease war and disarm themselves. His speech was humble, sincere, and non-political. He called for world-wide religious liberty, an idea which was precisely what the debate in the council had a difficult time supporting. Coming from the lips of the pope—for the first time in history—it was well received. On the question of peace, the Holy Father said in a voice that could be heard around the world, "War no more! War never again! It is peace, peace that must guide the destiny of the peoples of the world and of all humanity."

His trip was couched in ecumenical gestures, including a remarkable farewell message from the patriarch of Constantinople whom the pope had met the previous year in Palestine. Second, the council itself took up a discussion of that section of the Constitution on the Church in the Modern World, which dealt with **"the community of nations and the building up of peace."**

October 5, 1965 ▶ **Pope Paul returned** jubilantly from his brief trip to the United Nations and was received by the entire assembly of council fathers. His triumphant appearance on the world's stage and the more congenial discussion on Schema 13 added to the generally optimistic mood of the council. The council then set to work on that section dealing with world peace. Cardinal Ottaviani, who had spent his life in support of peace, spoke emphatically, saying that "War must be completely outlawed." He received warm applause from the council fathers, the first of the council for him. Nonetheless, some bishops argued that a "just war" could still be considered, and so the debate went on.

Meanwhile, voting was occurring almost daily on various parts of other documents, including the duties of bishops, the renewal of religious life, seminary training, Christian education, and non-Christian religions. A sense of urgency had emerged among the council fathers as this fourth period moved along.

As the debate on the Church in the Modern World came to its end, there was near-unanimous agreement that it should outrightly **condemn war** and the keeping of nuclear arms.

Perhaps the most significant element in the Constitution on the Church in the Modern World was **its call for the church to be in dialogue with people outside itself**, in the society and culture around us. In a voice that seemed opposite of Pius IX's *Syllabus of Errors*, the council said in so many words that the church could learn from others. The church, it said, "can enter into communion with different forms of culture, thereby enriching both itself and the cultures…"

October 7, 1965 ▶ The debate on **missionary activity** was taken up once again. At this point in the history of the church, the bishops understood they were moving from colonialism and imperialism to a new setting in which the Catholic communities in developing nations were now young churches that existed in their own right. The older understanding of "the missions" had to do with sending first world missionaries to these nations, but at the time of the council, there was already a growing indigenous clergy. This document was seen as an excellent beginning in the development of a new approach.

October 11, 1965 ▶ The pope announced to the council that **he was reserving to himself the right to decide any change in the law about celibacy for priests.** He sent a letter in which he said he did not wish to infringe in any way on the right of any of the council fathers to express themselves but that he did not deem a public discussion of celibacy to be a good thing and that anyone who wished to give an opinion should submit it to him in writing. He thus removed this from the council's agenda. His action met with the general approval of most council fathers.

On the same day ▶ The document on seminary training passed overwhelmingly.

On the same day ▶ **Archbishop Hallinan** of Atlanta called for a much-expanded role for women in the church.

October 14–15, 1965 ▶ Voting took place on **the schema dealing with non-Christian religions** (*Nostra Aetate*)**,** This document had three goals: (1) to stress the close scriptural ties between Christians and Jews, (2) to end the old accusation of deicide often hurled against the entire Jewish people, and (3) to end Christian anti-Semitism. Pope John's idea originally, this document was introduced in the first period and was solely about the Jews. It was then temporarily tagged onto the Decree on Ecumenism in the second period, but it did not meet with the approval of the council fathers on either of those attempts.

Now part of a larger document dealing with Hindus, Buddhists, and Muslims in addition to the Jews, there was still a group of more cautious bishops organized against the document. Nonetheless, it passed by a vote of 1,763 to 250.

October 14, 1965 ▶ Debate finally began on **the schema on priestly life and ministry**, the final document the council would consider. Because no discussion on celibacy was allowed, the document dealt only with less organic matters in the priesthood. Of course, the Eastern Catholic Churches in union with Rome were present, and theirs is a priesthood of mainly married men.

Background

It should be noted that the council fathers explicitly and intentionally moved away in this document (on the life and ministry of priests) from a term used to describe priesthood since the Middle Ages: *sacerdos* in Latin. This is a term that refers mainly to the powers of the priest to forgive sins, confect the Eucharist, and anoint the sick. The new term used in this document is broader and more pastoral, *presbyter*. This term was used in the New Testament and the early church to describe a threefold role—the same three-fold role assigned to all the baptized who are in the "common priesthood." Those roles are to be (1) priest or one who prays, (2) prophet or one who teaches, and (3) servant-king or one who governs.

The "common priesthood" or priesthood of the faithful refers to the fact that every baptized Christian is baptized as a priest, prophet, and servant-king. We say, therefore, that each baptized Christian has been baptized into this three-fold ministry. This is not, however, the same as the ministerial priesthood, which is a separate sacrament designated by ordination.

October 16, 1965 ▶ **Council debate formally ended** with the close of the discussion on the Decree of the Life and Ministry of Priests. This left time before the close of the fourth period and the entire council to complete work on already debated texts. A week's recess began, although work on polishing and finalizing the various documents continued behind the scenes.

It should be noted that by this point, the council fathers were exhausted, having heard more than 2,000 speeches, having sat through many tense moments, having endured the tedium of long presentations in Latin, and having taken part in countless debates on hundreds of ideas and proposals. They needed a rest.

October 25, 1965 ▶ **The council resumed its business,** dealing with unfinished schemas in preparation for voting on them. Council fathers worked informally with their *periti* and each other to complete work, debating and phrasing critical passages of the remaining documents, especially the Declaration on Religious Liberty and the Constitution on the Church in the Modern World. Suggestions made during the debates were taken under consideration by the various commissions responsible for preparing the multiple schemas. This was also an opportunity for the council fathers to take up minor points and lobby for their inclusion.

October 28, 1965 ▶ Five documents were approved and promulgated by Pope Paul VI. The final voting was decisive once again:
- **The Declaration on Non-Christian Religions:**
  2,221 to 88
- **The Decree on the Pastoral Duties of Bishops:**
  2,319 to 2
- **The Decree on the Renewal of Religious Life:**
  2,321 to 4
- **The Decree on Priestly Formation:**
  2,318 to 3
- **The Declaration on Christian Education:**
  2,290 to 35

October 29, 1965 ▶ The **Dogmatic Constitution on Divine Revelation** was sent to Pope Paul for promulgation. The final negotiations on this document were followed closely by the pope who sent a letter to the commission doing the work asking them to include Cardinal Bea in the discussions—because of his close ties to the other Christian Churches—and asking them to reconsider the text in order to reach a broader consensus on three things: the relation of Scripture to tradition, the question of biblical freedom from error, and the use of historic criticism related to the Gospels.

Background

It was a significant challenge for the council fathers to find a formula of words to express **the relationship between Scripture on the one hand and sacred tradition on the other.** In the end, in article nine of the Constitution, they provided a simply-worded explanation. Tradition serves the task of being faithful to Scripture, although "it is not from Sacred Scripture alone that the Church draws her certainty about everything which has been revealed." In the end, Scripture and tradition form one source of divine revelation, not two.

It should be noted that Pope John XXIII put this more simply. "One day, in speaking with a close confidant, he [Pope John] expressed his grief that so many women and men of goodwill thought that the Church rejected and condemned them. "But I must be like Christ," he said, referring to the crucifix on his desk. "I open wide my arms to embrace them. I love them, and I am their father. I am always ready to welcome them." Then turning to his guest, he said, "All that the Gospel requires of us has not yet been understood."[29] With these simple words, Pope John helped us all understand that God has not gone silent but is still speaking to us both in the consciences of the faithful and through the teaching ministry of the church.

It should be noted that, in the final wording of the texts of council documents, especially the one on divine revelation, the revisions were mainly in the hands of the members of the curia who were part of that small and very cautious group who opposed most reform and most of the work of the council. Experts representing most of the rest of the bishops of the world (and it was a vast majority!) scrutinized the work of this curial minority very carefully and often found errors of translation or wording that provided subtle, but significant, changes to the texts. These experts—representing most of the world's bishops—were able to do what many of the world's bishops did not have the theological expertise to do, which was to keep the agreed texts intact.

After the discussion on divine revelation, **the council fathers began their second recess** in order to provide rest and a time to refine and complete the documents still under question.

November 9, 1965 ▶ **The council resumed** its regular daily general congregations.

On this same day ▶ The historic **Decree on the Apostolate of the Laity** was sent to the pope for promulgation. This would be the first document of an ecumenical council to deal with the place of lay people in the life and ministry of the church. After the document had been printed, Pope Paul sent a dozen minor changes which he wanted in it. It should be noted that throughout this period, Pope Paul continued to play a strong hand in the development of the documents. Leaders tried to shield him somewhat from criticism (after the strong reaction to him in the third period for the same kind of interventions), but it was often clear—as in this case—that his "red pencil" had been active once again.

Indulgences

A **report on indulgences** was presented by a special commission set up by Pope Paul VI to study the issue. The report was issued as a "non-conciliar" document but was released as "a convenience" since the council fathers were all in Rome. The report began as an attempt on the part of the pope to experiment with the new synod of bishops, but the curia undermined that experiment, and this report was issued instead.

The report on indulgences was long, and it essentially **retained the status quo regarding their nature**, offering only minor reforms in the indulgence system. Protestant observers were somewhat shocked to see this—since the preaching of indulgences had been a significant factor that led Luther to his protest. But the Eastern Catholic Churches were also shocked since the document seemed to claim that indulgences had been active in the church since the apostolic period. Maximos Saigh, the elderly but unwavering leader from the East, blasted the document pointing out correctly that indulgences were an invention of the medieval church in the West with no connection to either Scripture or the early church. In the end, the document did reform the system, reducing the number of plenary indulgences available, and doing away with measuring indulgences in days or years. Speaking for many, Fr. Gregory Baum of Canada said, "Some of us are pained that indulgences should be raised at this moment in what, for lack of a stronger word, can be called an inadequate document."

November 15, 1965 ▶ Those council fathers who wanted the Constitution on the Church in the Modern World to outrightly **condemn communism** made a last, determined attempt to amend the text of the schema to include it. The petition to include the condemnation was considered by the commission and denied. A note referring to past condemnations was inserted instead.

November 18, 1965 ▶ Two more documents were promulgated today. The votes are as follows:
- **The Constitution on Divine Revelation:**
    2,344 to 6
- **The Decree on the Lay Apostolate:**
    2,305 to 2.

November 24, 1965 ▶ When the commission completing the revisions in the Constitution on the Church in the Modern World turned its attention to **the section on marriage,** the group experienced a **bombshell.** Pope Paul, once again using his "red pencil," sent a letter through his secretary of state, Archbishop Felici, requiring that certain items be included in this section, which would have the effect of solidifying the church's position relative to **birth control and the dignity of sexual intercourse.** Some members of the commission were delighted while others were both exasperated and angry. In the following days, the commission, led by Cardinal Dearden of Detroit, Michigan, and on the strength of a clarification from Pope Paul, succeeded in softening the impact of this conservative tactic in a way that met with the pope's personal approval.

Also, during this week, much discussion was held about the section on **war, nuclear war, and conscientious objection to war** in the same constitution (Church in the Modern World). In the end, the right to self-defense was maintained, and a delicate balancing of the interests of various nations regarding military power was sought.

December 4, 1965 ▶ Pope Paul took part in an **interdenominational Liturgy of the Word** at The Church of St. Paul's Outside-the-Walls, the very church where John XXIII had earlier announced his intention to call the council. This was the first time since the Reformation—the first time in history, therefore—that a pope prayed in this way with Protestants. Paul VI took his place among them with very little of the fanfare that usually accompanies papal ceremonies. In his remarks, the pope said, "We would like to have you with us always." More than 1,000 bishops attended even though a small number of others objected. The symbolism of this act was tremendous.

December 6, 1965 ▶ Pope Paul issued a *motu proprio* inaugurating **the reform of the curia,** long-awaited in the council. The name Supreme Congregation of the Holy Office —alarming to many because of its connections with the inquisitions of the past—was changed to Congregation for the Doctrine of the Faith (CDF). The newly-organized office would be less concerned, the pope said, with hunting for heretics and more concerned with promoting theological investigation. Finally, those whose teachings and writings were still under question would no longer be condemned without being allowed to make their case according to published norms.

On this same day ▶ The council also approved the **Constitution entitled The Church in the Modern World** with an overwhelming majority and sent it to the pope for promulgation.

December 7, 1965 ▶ A joint declaration from both Pope Paul VI and Orthodox Patriarch Athenagoras I was read simultaneously in Rome and in Istanbul, **lifting the ex-communication** they had jointly placed on one another in 1054. In so doing, they also invited the whole world to follow suit and to enter into greater unity. When the representative of the patriarch knelt to kiss the ring of the pope, Paul graciously raised him up and embraced him in a kiss of peace instead. As the patriarchal representative turned to leave the papal chair, a loud ovation of applause greeted him.

On this same day ▶ Final voting on the remaining documents occurred as well as their promulgation. The results were again decisive:

- **The Declaration on Religious Liberty:**
       2,308 to 70
- **The Decree on Missions:**
       2,394 to 5
- **The Constitution on the Church in the Modern World:**
       2,309 to 75
- **The Decree on Priestly Life and Ministry:**
       2,390 to 4

December 8, 1965 ▶ **The fourth period of Vatican II ended, and the council was officially closed** at an open-air Mass in the piazza in front of St. Peter's Basilica. The crowd that day may have numbered more than a quarter-million people from all faiths and all corners of the world. Pope Paul's words to them were warm and invitational. No one is a stranger to us, he said, no one is excluded from the love of the church, and no one is distant from us. The entire closing Mass was carried on international television as all the bells in Rome rang out their joy at the conclusion of this great council.

Briefly Annotated Summary[30] of the Documents of Vatican II

Foundational Documents
Constitutions on Liturgy and Revelation

Dogmatic Constitution on DIVINE REVELATION
In Latin: *Dei Verbum*. Approved on Nov 18, 1965. Vote: 2,344 to 6.

Here are some key points:
- God has chosen to reveal himself to us and to speak with us as friends.
- Revelation is complete in Jesus who is the Christ, but what the Scriptures demand of us is still being revealed each and every day. Jesus is the source of all revelation. The Scriptures, therefore, are the foundation of divine revelation and tradition elaborates the meaning of the Scriptures for each generation.
- Doctrine and dogma are expressed in different words for different generations. But the eternal truths do not change.
- Dated routine changes, but authentic tradition remains always with us.
- Our response to God's revelation is faith. Through faith, we entrust our whole selves to God. This faith is handed on to all generations through living traditions.
- There is a close link between Scripture, Tradition, and the teaching authority of the Church.
- Revelation is handed on to us by the Church.
- God wants us to know him fully!
- God reveals the inner life of the Trinity to us, communicating God's own self to us. This is known to us as grace.
- Over time, there is growth in our understanding of what God desires
- This growth in understanding is expressed in our sacred Tradition. So, Tradition and Scripture have a very close connection and flow from the same divine well.

Constitution on SACRED LITURGY
In Latin: *Sacrosanctum Concilium.* Approved on Dec 4, 1963.
Vote: 2,147 to 4.

Here are some key points:
- The bishops wanted to give vigor to the Christian life of the faithful; to adapt what is changeable to the needs of today, to promote union among all who believe in Jesus who is the Christ, and to strengthen the church's mission to all humankind.
- This document established that the Mass (liturgy) is the source and summit of the Christian life.
- It said that, for the liturgy to be effective, the faithful must be well disposed, know what they are doing, and participate.
- It established that some elements are changeable (language, books, prayers, music, persons, and places), and some aren't (Scripture, bread, wine, offertory, consecration, communion).
- It allowed for the use of the vernacular in worship. Latin was retained officially, but for full participation to become a reality, the language of the people would be needed.
- It restored the Eucharist as an act rather than a static devotional object. This meant a downplaying of devotions outside of Mass (rosary, benediction, and so forth) to focus on the liturgical year and rites.
- It established Baptism and Eucharist with primacy among the sacraments.
- It called for the full, active, conscious participation of all the faithful as the aim to be considered before all others.
- It reminds us it is never enough to simply follow the "letter of the law," making sure we are correct and proper.
- It allowed for the removal of elements that are "out of harmony with the inner nature of the liturgy."
- It proposed a list of reforms, including simpler rites, more use of the Bible, the prayer of the faithful, roles for the laity, and others.

Core Documents on the Church
Constitutions on the Church *ad intra* and *ad extra*

The Dogmatic Constitution on THE CHURCH
In Latin: *Lumen Gentium.* Approved on Nov 21, 1964.
Vote: 2,151 to 5.

Here are some key points:
- The church is in Jesus who is the Christ; it is a sacrament of the Christ, a mystery of depth.
- It is the Body of Jesus, who is the Christ.
- It is the People of God, among whom the baptized are called to be ministers.
- It is led by the bishops, bound as a college, in unity with the pope, in a bond of charity and peace.
- The primary role of the bishop is to shepherd God's people. The ministry of the bishop is that of a servant to the people of God.
- The permanent diaconate is restored.
- There is a distinction between the "priesthood of the baptized" and that of the "ordained."
- For those called to be Catholic, the Church is necessary for salvation. But merely following the law of the Church is not enough; we must also live in love.
- Those in other Christian churches are also related to us. Likewise, Jews, Moslems, and all who seek God are connected to us.
- The role of the faithful is to be the church in the world. We are to seek the Reign of God in our everyday work.
- The call to holiness is universal, and the way to holiness is love.
- Religious men and women live as dedicated members.
- We are part of the great "communion of saints" bound together in God's love.
- The Blessed Virgin Mary takes her place, too, among God's people, and all devotion to her must ultimately lead to Jesus, who is the Christ and our Lord.

Pastoral Constitution
on the CHURCH IN THE MODERN WORLD
In Latin: *Gaudium et Spes*. Approved on Dec 7, 1965.
Vote: 2,309 to 75.

Here are some key points:
- "The joys and hopes, the griefs and anxieties of the people of this age, especially those who are poor or in any way afflicted, these are the joys and hopes, the grief and anguish of the followers of Christ."
- We must look at and trust the signs of the times and understand the world in which we live. (Contrast with Pius IX's Syllabus of Errors in 1864: The pope "cannot and should not be reconciled and come to terms with progress, liberalism, and modern civilization...")
- All human persons have dignity and are our responsibility.
- Deep within our conscience, we detect a truth that we have not laid upon ourselves but that we must follow. It's voice, ever calling us to love and to do what is right and avoid evil sounds in our hearts at the right moment. For we have in our hearts a law inscribed by God. Our conscience is our most secret core and our sanctuary. There we are alone with God whose voice echoes in our depths.
- Everyone must consider his or her neighbor as "another self."
- We should have respect and love for those who think differently than we do.
- The church lives and acts in the world. "Let there be no false opposition between professional and social activities on the one part and religious life on the other." It isn't "the world against the church." It's "the world together with the church."
- We must all seek the common good.
- We have an inborn hunger for God.
- Treated problems of "special urgency": Households of faith, culture, economics, politics, & war and peace. Called all to support and seek the common good.

Documents on the People of God
Bishops, Priests, Laity, and Religious

Decree on THE BISHOPS' PASTORAL OFFICE
In Latin: *Christus Dominus*. Approved on Oct 28, 1965.
Vote: 2,319 to 2.

Here are some key points:
- Over time the church developed a dominant central leader, the pope, and a powerful set of central offices, the Roman Curia. Bishops' powers were whittled down to almost nothing and they functioned as "branch offices" of the central Roman bureau.
- There were no connections among bishops, even within a given nation.
- There was very little sense of the universal church as such, and more an understanding of the Roman church with a powerful reach from its curia.
- This document speaks, however, of the bishops' shared or collegial responsibility for the whole church and says that it is expressed by the institution of a synod of bishops together with the pope.
- It directs that these synods should be composed of representatives elected by local conferences of bishops. Therefore, such conferences should be established on national or regional levels.
- These local conferences may reorganize dioceses, move the bishops' sees to a more suitable location, and collaborate with other conferences to meet regional challenges.
- The Roman Curia is ordered to increase the number of diocesan bishops and laypeople in its membership.
- Offices of the Roman Curia must reform specific procedures and return the authority for ordinary, everyday administrative matters to bishops.
- Each diocesan bishop has independent and immediate authority for his own see; they should set up boards of consultants to meet the needs of the day. And they are to establish

pastoral councils made up of priests and laypeople to help them govern. Parishes are also required to create pastoral councils.
- Overall, this was something of a follow-up document to the chapter on bishops in the Constitution on the Church. Its primary purpose is to give a job description for the bishop and stress the need for shared decision making (collegiality).
- It calls for bishops to be servant leaders rather than princes: "The bishop stands among his people as one who serves," it says.

Decree on APOSTOLATE OF THE LAITY
In Latin: *Apostolicam Actuositatem*. Approved on Nov 18, 1965. Vote: 2,305 to 2.

Here are some key points:
- Before the council, the view of the church was very clerical, meaning that the clergy had prerogatives that laypeople did not. Laymen and women were given only a passive role which they were expected to accept with complete obedience.
- At that time, laypeople were called "subject" much as you would expect in a feudal system. They were not seen as the foundation of the church.
- The term 'church' often simply meant the clergy.
- But this document, flowing as it does from the chapter on the laity in the Constitution on the Church, declares that laypeople have ministries of their own by virtue of their baptisms, not merely a sharing in the ministry of the ordained.
- Lay women and men were recognized in this document as fully responsible members of the People of God. This new definition of the church as the People of God placed lay people in an entirely new position.
- Lay people were seen to have a much larger share of self-determination in the modern world. Lay people actually share in the universal priesthood and in the gifts of the Holy Spirit. This Spirit, as is well known, blows where it wants. It calls people in their consciences as it pleases.
- The document calls on the hierarchy to regard lay people with great trust, to seek their advice and counsel, and to

think of them as a valued part of the church.

- Meanwhile, laypeople are obliged to be witnesses to Jesus and the church in their own sphere of influence, shaping and animating the world with the spirit of Jesus who is the Christ.
- And finally, laypeople, like all baptized Christians, must "preach" the word of God at all times by their lifestyles, choices, and witness. Lay people may also collaborate with other Christians and even non-Christians.
- This is the first document in history addressed to laypeople by an ecumenical council.

Decree on THE MINISTRY AND LIFE OF PRIESTS
In Latin: *Presbyterorum Ordinis*. Approved on Dec 7, 1965. Vote: 2,390 to 4.

Here are some key points:
- The priesthood had become a clerical state, set aside from the laity.
- The focus of priesthood was on a sacred power to forgive sins, confect the Eucharist, and preside at all public prayer. He was the sole minister of the altar and the sacraments.
- The term in Latin used to describe the priest before the council was *sacerdos.*
- Priests were expected to live a scaled back monastic type of life, in obedience to the bishop, in the celibate state, and as part of a society of other priests.
- They were paid only a "stipend" and given "allowances" for their other needs such as cars, housekeepers, or education. They were also paid a stipend for presiding at the sacraments, especially for "saying Masses" for the dead. These allowances or stipends prevented them from having a professional salary as did their Protestant and Anglican counterparts.
- This document calls on priests to support the laity which is considered by the church to share in the one priesthood of Jesus who is the Christ.
- It employs a new term for the priest, *presbyter,* which is a biblical term and one used in the apostolic age of the church. It suggests service as "the first role" of the priest.

- It reaffirmed celibacy for priests of the Latin Rite while saying that celibacy is not demanded by the very nature of the priesthood but only that it seems "suitable." The question of celibacy for the Latin rite had been taken off the council's agenda by Pope Paul VI.
- Priests were called to holiness and to act as servants to their communities.
- The priest is not to be separated from laypeople but should stand with them in his life, work, and ministry.
- The document calls for the development of priestly piety, derived from priestly service within the world.
- Bishops are called in this document to listen to and work with their priests, forming a council of priests.
- The text goes out of its way to commend the married priests of the Eastern Catholic Churches.

Decree on THE ADAPTATION & RENEWAL of RELIGIOUS LIFE

In Latin: *Perfectae Caritatis*. Approved Oct 28, 1965.
Vote: 2,321 to 4.

Here are some key points:

- The founders of religious orders were often men and women of great vision. The purpose and mission of the various congregations of men and women religious were clear and responded to the culture and civilization of their day.
- They lived lives dedicated to holiness, praying together and formed by scripture on the one hand and by the needs of the age on the other.
- As the church grew and entered new areas of the world, many religious communities stepped forward to provide for temporary special needs.
- A side effect of this was that some religious orders lost touch with the vision and mission of their founders. The tried to meet the new needs of the age while continuing with ancient community practices, dress, and lines of authority.
- This document urges reform but leaves it to the individual orders to renovate themselves.
- They are encouraged to return to the sources of their original mission, especially to sacred scripture, the spirit of their founders, and the new needs of the contemporary world.
- On this basis, the document urges them to reform all outmoded forms of life. It encourages communities to act as a whole, not merely through their leaders.
- Any remaining class distinctions or sense of being a "subject" were to be eliminated. Members were no longer expected to live in a state of spiritual dependency.
- Orders which no longer have a purpose or mission may not accept any new candidates.
- It does not repeat the teaching of Trent that religious life is a superior state to that of the married.

Documents on the Mission of the Church
Education, Missionary work, Communications, Training Priests

Decree on the Media of Social COMMUNICATIONS
In Latin: *Inter Mirifica*. Approved on Dec 4, 1963.
Vote: 1,960 to 164.

Here are some key points:
- Church leaders often mistrusted the modern so-called "mass media."
- The media was considered a source of immorality.
- This document speaks about the importance of press, film, radio, and television for help in preaching the Word.
- It calls for guidelines to be developed for its proper use.
- It calls all producers of media to a higher level, but the tone of this was condescending.
- Lay people were identified as the ones more heavily counted on to staff the church's own media and to review public media.
- This document was written before mobile phones, the internet, wide-spread use of personal computers, or other modern means of communication, so it is seen as out of touch in today's environment.

Decree on PRIESTLY TRAINING
In Latin: *Optatam Totius*. Approved on Oct 28, 1965.
Vote: 2,318 to 3.

Here are some key points:
- The first seminaries were established pretty much throughout the Western church within several decades after the Council of Trent, even though Trent had not meant to demand that.
- The early seminaries in most places provided a life of monastic seclusion because they were modeled on the monastic tradition. Living in that way did not help develop the personalities and growth to adulthood needed for seminarians. They stressed obedience and skills, and put doctrinal learning over the development of human virtues.
- The teaching was abstract and often aimed at a rather apologetic approach against the church's supposed enemies (such as the Protestants or Anglicans) by aggressive claims against them and by undermining the opposing position.
- Manuals to assure uniform and standard formation among all seminaries were created and followed religiously.
- This document gave freedom to local bishops' conferences to organize seminaries that would better meet their needs.
- It called for seminaries to adapt to modern pastoral needs and called for courses in pastoral counseling, ecumenism, history, and personal formation.
- It stressed that biblical piety should replace the rubrical piety which had dominated prior to the council. Toward this end, it promoted as a priority the study of the Bible and biblical theology. The old manuals did not have such courses.
- It taught that the views of others, including those who disagree with us, may no longer be presented only in their negative aspect.
- It called for a great deal more contact between seminarians and people in the world, especially to understand the pastoral needs of modern women and men.
- It required that more opportunities be provided for personality development, the skills of teamwork, and ways of thinking outside of rigid, scholastic ways of thought.

Decree on MISSIONARY ACTIVITY

In Latin: *Ad Gentes*. Approved on Dec 7, 1965. Vote: 2,394 to 5.

Here are some key points:

- Most of the missionary activity of the church was focused on baptizing "pagans" to prevent them from suffering eternal damnation. Baptism was seen as a sort of magical sacrament whose primary purpose was to remove original sin.
- Missionary activity occurred during a period when northern nations colonized and imperialized the rest of the world.
- Therefore, missionary activity also brought with it a European way of living.
- Various Christian denominations competed with each other for "converts," causing great scandal and making Christianity difficult to believe.
- In this document, people who practice non-Christian religions received more esteem and trust. They were given much more understanding.
- In particular, the non-European cultural values of these people were sincerely respected. Indeed, missionaries were called on to root their work in these local, indigenous cultures, looking to them as a way of learning new perspectives on scripture. They were encouraged to retain local, "pagan" religious customs and incorporate the gospel into them, a radical idea.
- Missionaries were encouraged to establish friendly relations with other Christian missionaries, providing a common witness to Jesus who is the Christ in their everyday lives.
- The bishops at the council asked that a commission on missions be established, made up of bishops and experts whose purpose would be to exercise a decisive influence on the activities of the office of the curia known as the Congregation for the Propagation of Faith.
- Also states that the whole church is missionary, meaning that all the people of God are called to introduce others to the faith, a point later emphasized by Pope Francis in *The Joy of the Gospel*.

Declaration on CHRISTIAN EDUCATION

In Latin: *Gravissimum Educationis*. Approved on Oct 28, 1965. Vote: 2,290 to 35.

Here are some key points:
- In some parts of the church, it was mandatory to send children to Catholic schools. However, they were too few in number and unable to compete well with public schools. They were also focused too much on "preserving truth" rather than on developing minds.
- In this document, parents are named as the primary educators of their own children. Therefore, the educational obligations of parents get the primary emphasis.
- For the first time, the church recognized the state's right to play a vital role in education.
- The right of the Catholic Church to maintain schools continued to be emphasized.
- The document teaches that Catholic schools should accept non-Catholic students.
- It also urges that more attention be paid to Catholic students in non-Catholic schools.
- Overall, this document was judged in post-conciliar years to be a weak document that left most of the work to post-conciliar development.

Documents on the External Relations of the Church

Religious Liberty, Eastern Catholics, Ecumenism, Non-Christians

Decree on ECUMENISM

In Latin: *Unitatis Redintegratio*. Approved on Nov 21, 1964. Vote: 2,137 to 11.

Here are some key points:

- Sought a restoration of ties rather than demanding that other Christians simply "return to Rome."
- For the first time, it admits that the blame for separation was on both sides.
- Called for a change of heart to make ecumenism possible.
- Said that sharing in worship may, at times, be necessary to gain the grace of unity.
- Encouraged dialogue and calls for the Roman Church to reform itself as part of the process of reunion.
- Based on a real effort here to understand other Christians and make the Church's position understandable to them.
- The shared Christian heritage and history were recognized, and the church as a whole was called to live up to this heritage.
- Non-Catholic Christians were recognized as churches and church communities in their own right.
- The Catholic church can learn something from these other Christians.
- The issues that separate us are not glossed over, but ways are sought to overcome divisions through common dialogue and more profound knowledge of scripture.
- Says that the shared desire for unity should be increased through common prayer and by avoiding all conflict and competition, especially in mission lands.

Decree on the
CATHOLIC CHURCHES OF THE EASTERN RITE
In Latin: *Orientalium Ecclesiarum*. Approved on Nov 21, 1964.
Vote: 2,110 to 39.

Here are some key points:
- Up to this time, these Eastern Churches were considered something of a relic of past ages. The much larger Roman/Latin rite tried to impose law, liturgy, its own doctrinal brand of theological thinking on them.
- These churches were much more mystical in tone and nature.
- But this document recognizes all the different parts of the church and sees them all equal in standing.
- Therefore, the document calls for the rights and individual approaches proper to these Eastern Churches to be restored and respected.
- These churches may also name their own bishops.
- The priesthood of the Eastern Catholic Churches was fully recognized, including a married clergy which they have always maintained.
- Members of those churches can, if they desire, receive the sacraments in Catholic churches, just as Catholic Christians may receive them in Orthodox churches when no Catholic priest is available.
- Marriages before an Orthodox priest are valid, and the joint use of churches is permitted.

Declaration on THE RELATION OF THE CHURCH
TO NON-CHRISTIANS
In Latin: *Nostra Aetate*. Approved on Oct 28, 1965.
Vote: 2,221 to 88.

Here are some key points:
- Catholic missions had been taking an almost purely negative stance against all non-Christian religions. They were seen only as targets for conversion.
- This harsh stance was even stronger in the case of the Moslems. They were considered militant "enemies" of the church in part because of their expansion into formerly Catholic nations such as Spain and others.

- Likewise, the Jews were considered an "obdurate people" because of their treatment of Jesus. Forgotten in this was the fact that many Jews also followed Jesus, and the early church was primarily composed of Jews. Jesus' entire family was Jewish, as were all of his apostles. However, this harsh Catholic attitude included a robust anti-Semitic strain which certainly fueled the persecution and murder of the Jews by the Nazis.
- This document was, therefore, earth-shaking in that it finally recognizes the activity of God in all religions. This new attitude was not seen as a threat to the conviction that the church was given the fullness of truth by and in Jesus who is the Christ.
- This document began as a statement only about our relations with the Jews but was widened to say that the truth can be found outside the Body of Christ and is to be respected wherever it is found, mentioning in particular Hinduism, Buddhism, and Islam, as well as Judaism.
- All people of every religion, therefore, deserve understanding and esteem.
- Furthermore, the document makes clear that the church is linked to the Moslems in as much as Moslems honor Jesus and the prophets.
- Likewise, the Church has a unique relationship with the Jews for the reasons just cited, but also because we share the Hebrew Scriptures and consider them sacred. The Jews were and still are God's chosen people; God does not go back on such a choice.
- The idea was emphasized in this document that Jews—in the first century and also today—are not collectively guilty for the death of Jesus. All anti-Semitism must be uprooted from the prayers of the church, from preaching, and from education.
- Toward this end, the document recommends that Jews and Christians share in common biblical studies.

Declaration on RELIGIOUS LIBERTY:
In Latin: *Dignitatis Humanae.* Approved on Dec 7, 1965.
Vote: 2,308 to 70.

Here are some key points:
- Before the council, "religious liberty as a human right" was seen as "relativistic" thinking—which meant that such thinking rejected what was considered the universal, objective truth that the Catholic Church alone had the right to teach the Gospel. It was therefore rejected by the popes and Roman curia. To them, only "real truth" could have rights and only the Catholic church had that truth.
- On this basis, the church was able to justify the condemnation and killing of many people who professed other faiths.
- Religious tolerance was allowed before the council but only as a "lesser evil." Still, Catholics were expected to reject error wherever it was found—and all Protestant thinking was in error.
- However, turning the tables a bit, wherever Catholics were in the minority, they worked for religious liberty. It was only when they constituted a majority that they claimed freedom for the Catholic religion alone.
- This document adjusted this thinking, much to the dismay of a small group of cautious bishops and bishops from mainly Catholic nations.
- Because of the dignity of the human person, the document says, everyone has the right to free exercise of religion, private and public, individually and collectively. No one may be coerced into faith.
- Because of this, no one should ever be prevented by force from practicing their religion or be discriminated against because of their faith. In other words, local government powers may not interfere in the church's business. This includes pastoral appointments, allowing people to gather as a parish, and allowing people to connect with others of their faith outside their own nation.
- Hence, religious liberty is a fundamental right and must be protected by the state.
- This was the most controversial of the council documents. It began life as a chapter in the document on ecumenism.

"It is one of the major tenets of Catholic doctrine that [our] response to God in faith must be free: no one, therefore, is to be forced to embrace the Christian faith against [their] own will."

- The church claimed freedom for itself in this document, but also for all religious practices of every kind everywhere.

Comprehensive Summaries
of the Four Constitutions

Liturgy

Church

Revelation

Church in the Modern World

The Constitution on the Sacred Liturgy

from the Second Vatican Council
promulgated by Pope Paul VI on December 4, 1963

Sacrosanctum Concilium

Introduction

1 We who are the participants in this,
    The Second Vatican Council,
      have a sense of both hope and urgency
        for the Church.
We desire much for the world and believe that the Church
      has much to offer to all people.
Therefore, in all the work that is set out before us,
    we intend to adhere to
      the following ideals:

First, the Christian life is to be lived with vigor.
      Our hope is that through the reform of this council,
      Christians may embrace the Christian faith
        more profoundly each day.

Second, our world has changed substantially in recent years.
      Where it is both possible and beneficial,
      we want the Church to change as well
      to serve the needs of our day more graciously.

Third, presently, Christians are not fully united.
      We want to nurture and promote everything
      that will help to bring about greater understanding
      and more authentic unity among all Christian people.

Fourth, the Church has much to offer humankind.
      We want to strengthen those elements of the Church
      which allow people to experience
        the deep love of God
      and the challenging call of Jesus.

Given these ideals
      and the reform that is already happening

in the Church,
we believe that now is the right time
to bring about reform
in the way we worship and pray.
We, therefore, want to reform the liturgy
and increase our fervor for it.

2 The essential work of redemption
is accomplished mainly through the liturgy,
especially the Eucharist.
This is true because it is through participation in the liturgy
that we are given everything that we need
to understand the mystery
of our relationship with Jesus, the Christ.
We are given the strength we need
to witness to the reality of Jesus in our lives
and in the life of the Church.

3 Jesus who is the Christ is intimately knowable
and is, at the same time, a mystery.
Hence, the Church is also at the same time
both understandable and incomprehensible.
The Church is both human and divine,
visible and invisible,
eager to act and intent on contemplation,
present in the world yet not entirely at home here.
The liturgy helps us to live with this tension
and thus, enter fully into a life of faith.
It is the liturgy which builds up those who are present
and is also a sign to those who are not.
The liturgy is an expression of our life in the Spirit
and a sign to the world of ultimate unity.
It enables those who participate
to reach full and conscious Christian maturity

4 We are, therefore, setting forth some ideals
under which the liturgy should be reformed
and by which it can be embraced fully
by the faithful.
We intend to outline the essential principles of liturgy
which should always be followed.
We will also establish some practical norms,

meant mainly for the Roman Rite
but also intended to be applied to the whole church when
appropriate.
The rites of the Catholic Church hold a particular dignity
and we want to preserve them.
We also want to revise these rites
so that, when celebrated with greater vigor,
they are better able to address the circumstances
of modern times.

Chapter I:
General Principles for Restoration and Promotion
of Sacred Liturgy

*I. The Nature of the Sacred Liturgy and Its Importance
in the Church's Life*

5 We believe that Jesus is the Christ,
which is to say, "the Anointed One of God."
So tangible was eternity in the person of Jesus
that those who encountered him
found themselves completely healed,
fully forgiven and totally united with God
and with each other.
It was as though they had crossed the threshold of eternity:
no longer slaves to the disappointments of time
but free to discover at every moment
the thread of eternity which holds all of life together.
They found that in this community of believers
there existed a new way of being in the world.
Freely reconciled in Jesus who is the Christ,
they were thus free to bring
their entire selves to the throne of God
and worship God in absolute humility and dignity.

All that Jesus gave to the human race
was principally achieved
through the Paschal Mystery.
When we speak of the Paschal Mystery
we refer to Jesus' profound death and burial,
his resurrection and sending of the apostles
to the world.
The Gospel of John gives us a vivid image
of the magnitude of this paschal mystery.

The Gospel writer tells how a spear was driven deep
    into Christ's heart as he waited upon the Cross.
From this noble heart,
    God's very life gushed forth upon the world: Eternity!
Christ's life drenched the whole earth that Friday afternoon.
    And like soft rain, it gave new life to the parched soil
        of humanity's heart.
This, we might say, is really when the Church was born.

6 For Jesus who is the Christ did not pour out his life for us
    just to leave us abandoned.
Instead, Jesus the Christ sent the Holy Spirit
    to fill the lives of the first apostles and disciples
    and to stir up in them the desire
    to live at the table of God's gracious love.
Thus, the first followers of Jesus
    were empowered to preach the good news

And God also gave those first disciples
    everything they would need
    to remain fully attentive to the mystery
        that they had experienced
        during Jesus' lifetime.
Thus, did they baptize those who came to believe
    in Jesus who is the Christ
    and in the saving power of his life and death.
Thus, too, did they share together the Eucharist,
    the full celebration of the presence of Jesus.
It was both in their loving actions and in their worship
    that the first disciples came to know
        their profound call to "be Church."
From that very first day until now
    we have never stopped announcing the Word,
        baptizing those who believe,
        and celebrating the Eucharist.
The early writings of Christians,
    contained mainly in our Bible,
    demonstrate this clearly.
The second chapter of *Acts of the Apostles*
    tells explicitly how those
        who believed the words of St. Peter were baptized.
They also continued steadfastly, the text tells us,

"in the communion of the breaking of bread
and in prayers..."
So today we continue in this holy tradition,
holding out hope that by doing so,
we, too, will come to know
the presence of Jesus, the Christ.

7 We have lost nothing for not having lived during the time
of Jesus' life on earth.
We have everything that the first disciples had
to help us believe in Jesus and live as though this faith
really makes a difference!
Yet that is precisely what Christ promised;
and, being faithful to that promise,
Jesus is always present in the Church.

This presence is most noticeable
in our liturgical celebrations,
In the Mass, Jesus who is the Christ is really present
in the ministry of the Church,
in the Eucharistic bread and wine,
in the proclaimed Word of God,
and in the whole community
gathered in song and prayer.
Jesus, the Christ is also present in a unique way
in all the other sacraments.
Because of Jesus, the Christ's assured presence,
the liturgy gives us the unique opportunity
to enter fully and honestly into
our most authentic relationship with God.
Hence, the liturgy is the most sacred act of human life.
Nothing more significant is ever done.

8 The liturgy is really a celebration of eternity
here and now.
It contains the entire mystery of faith:
it is our food as pilgrims, our hymn of praise,
and our hope for a partnership with God.
The sacred liturgy gathers together
all who have gone before us
and all who will come after us
together with Jesus who is the Christ,

the Alpha and the Omega.

9 But even though liturgy is most essential to us,
        it is not all we do as members of the Church.
Various ministries and activities of the Church
        help to give witness to the truth of Jesus' presence
            in the whole world.
The ministry of preaching and teaching
        helps those who have not yet heard the word of God
        to experience the first stirring of faith
            and the pull of eternity at their hearts.
Preaching and teaching also helps
        those who already follow Jesus, the Christ
        to grasp more firmly and clearly
        the mysteries of the faith they are trying to live.
Other ministries of service and compassion
        within both the Church and the world
        show clearly the call of the Christian
            to be the light of the world.

10 Nevertheless, the liturgy is the summit toward which
        the Christian life is directed
        and the very source of that life to begin with.
It is a fount from which grace is poured over us,
        and it is that place to which we go
                for reconciliation, peace, and communion.
Among all liturgical celebrations,
        the Eucharist, of course, holds a special prominence.
In the Eucharist, the eternal covenant
        between God and humankind is renewed,
        and Jesus' love is rekindled in us.
11 Precisely because it is so central to us,
        and so crucial in the Christian journey,
        the faithful who come to liturgy
            must be well disposed,
            ready to participate,
            and actively engaged in the rites.
It is not enough simply to follow the letter of the law,
        making sure that our liturgies
        are "correct" and "proper."
Much more is required of those
        who practice liturgical leadership:

they also have to ensure that participants
have the opportunity to take part fully,
to understand what they are doing,
and to be enriched by its effects.
12 We do realize that participating in the liturgy
is not all that is required for the spiritual life.
There is also the need for private prayer
and witness to the life-giving death of Jesus.
13 Therefore, popular devotions and all practices
which help to foster a richer
and more authentic faith life are encouraged.
Such devotions, however, should be in harmony
with the liturgical season
and always draw people more deeply
into the celebration of the sacred liturgy.

II. The Promotion of Liturgical Instruction and Active Participation

14 Because of their baptisms,
all the faithful have both a right and a duty
to full and active participation in the liturgy.
Participation in the liturgy can be seen as a "right"
because without it
a person would experience spiritual starvation.
It is a "duty" because without the liturgy,
Christian people cannot live the life
to which God calls them.
In this sense, liturgy is as fundamental as food and clothing.

Therefore, we the participants
in this Second Vatican Council
propose one guiding principle before all others
as we approach the question
of restoring and reforming the sacred liturgy.
The principle is this:
In the restoration and promotion of the sacred liturgy
the full and active participation by all the people
is the aim to be considered
before all else!
We realize that if the ideal
of full and active participation by all people
is ever to be achieved,
then liturgical leaders, particularly pastors,

must be absolutely and internally convinced
of the spirit and power of the liturgy.
In this way, they can pass on such fervor
to all the faithful entrusted to their ministry.

15 Therefore, professors appointed to teach in seminaries
and institutes of pastoral education
must be adequately trained.
16 In seminaries, the study of the liturgy
is to be ranked among the compulsory courses.
The liturgy in all its dimensions:
theological, historical, spiritual, practical, and legal
is to be fully explored.
All seminary course work should connect itself
to the liturgy.
17 Seminarians are also required
to be formed in liturgical piety,
celebrating the mysteries
and observing the liturgical year.
18 Those priests already working in the field
are to be offered updated training now.
19 And all the faithful should likewise be provided updating
taking into account their age and condition,
their way of life and religious culture,
so they may become active participants.
20 The use of the media to transmit the rites
should be done with discretion and dignity.

III. The Reform of the Sacred Liturgy

21 So that the faithful may more certainly derive
an abundance of graces,
the Church now undertakes a general restoration
of the sacred liturgy.
The liturgy is composed of elements
which cannot be changed.
But there have also crept in among these
other elements which are out of harmony
with the inner nature of the liturgy
and are, therefore, unsuited for it.
We are restoring both texts and rites
so they more clearly express
the holy things which they signify.

A) General Norms

22 As we begin to move toward restoration of the liturgy,
  we pause to remind all
  (1) that the regulation of the liturgy
    is the proper work of the Pope
    and sometimes also the local bishop.
(2) Within certain defined limits, the regulation of the liturgy
  also belongs to various local bodies of bishops
  who set forth norms for their regions.
    (3) Others should not make changes.
23 When implementing change,
  consider carefully and first
  any theological, historical, or pastoral aspects of it.
Take into account recent experiences,
  recent liturgical norms, and the good of the Church.
In most cases, reforms should grow from existing customs.
  Care should be taken
  that significant differences in style
  do not exist within a single region.
24 The Scriptures are of the highest importance
  to the liturgical celebration,
  so care should be taken in proclaiming them,
    homilizing on them,
    singing hymns derived from them,
    or praying inspired by them.
A warm and living love of the Scriptures is to be fostered.
25 The liturgical books are to be revised
  as soon as possible,
  employing experts and consulting the bishops.

*B. Norms drawn from the hierarchic and communal nature
of the Liturgy*

26 We are reminded that liturgical services
  are not private functions
  but celebrations of the whole church.
Therefore, liturgical services are a concern
  to the whole Church
  but especially to those whose role
  by virtue of their rank, office, or participation
    are affected.
27 So whenever rites have a communal nature,

they should be set in a communal setting,
                    not in a private one.
This is especially true of the Mass and sacraments.
28 Anyone with a part of the rite to perform
        should do all of, but only
        that which pertains to his or her role.
29 Servers, lectors, commentators, and members of the choir
        exercise a genuine liturgical function
        and should do so with piety and decorum.
                    They must, therefore, be well trained.
30 The laypeople should take an active role as well
        by acclamations, responses, songs, and actions,
        as well as by their posture.
                At the proper times,
                a reverent silence should be observed.
31 As the liturgical books are revised,
        the people's parts should be included.
32 The liturgy makes clear who has what role,
        as well as the place of the ordained,
        and allows for the recognition of civil authorities,
                    but no individual honors are to be paid
                    in the liturgy to private persons or classes.

C) Norms based upon the didactic and pastoral nature
of the Liturgy
33 The sacred liturgy is both worship of God
        as well as instruction for the faithful.
In the liturgy, God speaks to the people
        and Jesus proclaims the Good News.
                The people reply to God
                in both song and prayer.
34 Therefore, the rites should be distinguished
        by a noble simplicity;
        they should be short, clear,
                and unencumbered by repetitions.
Explanation of their meaning should not be necessary.

35 In order that the connection
        between words and rites is clear,
        these principles should be followed:
(1) There is to be more reading from Scripture,
        with more variance and suitability.

(2) Sermons should be drawn mainly
    from scripture and liturgy
    and should proclaim God's beautiful works,
        the mystery of Jesus
        and the wonderful moments
            which we share together at Mass.
(3) Liturgical instruction itself should be brief
    and should not intrude on the rites.
(4) Bible services are encouraged,
    especially on vigils or when no priest is present.

36 Concerning the language used in liturgy,
(1) The use of Latin is preserved
        (2) but the use of the mother tongue
    which may be of great advantage to the people
        is also permitted
    when it is (3) requested by the local bishops.
(4) Translations into the mother tongue must be approved.

D) Norms for adapting the Liturgy to the culture and traditions
of peoples
37 The church does not wish to impose a rigid uniformity
        in matters where it is not necessary
        and, therefore, local customs may be introduced
            into the liturgy
            provided they aren't based in superstition.
38 Therefore, provisions for adaptations of this sort
        shall be made
        making sure the unity of the Church is preserved.
39 Such adjustments
        for different groups, regions, and peoples
        shall be drawn up and approved by the local bishops
        and must follow the fundamental norms
            of this Constitution.
40 When more extensive adaptations are needed
        and these are the norms for those occasions:
(1) The local bishops should consider carefully
        what to include
        and then submit those ideas to the Holy See.
(2) The Holy See will then guide the local church to
        proper experimentation
            over a suitable period of time.

(3) Experts on liturgy should be consulted.

E) Promotion of Liturgical Life in Diocese and Parish

41 The local bishop is essentially the "high priest"
       of the diocese and, with the local priests,
       they form one priesthood
       with the full active participation of the people.
42 But because it's impossible for a diocese to exist
       of one parish,
       parish priests take the place of the bishop
       so that the liturgical life of the parish
             can be fostered above all else.
Such parishes constitute a full expression of the church
       and are not mere geographic divisions.

F) The Promotion of Pastoral-Liturgical Action

43 We hereby call for all to enter into
       the promotion and restoration of the liturgy with zeal!
44 Toward this end, national liturgical commissions
       are to be established
       "consisting of persons who are eminent
             in these matters,
             and including lay [people]."
These commissions should foster
       vigorous pastoral-liturgical action,
       especially in local dioceses, groups of dioceses,
             and parishes.
45 Likewise, each diocese should have a similar commission
       to assist the bishops
       to regulate pastoral liturgical action,
       promote study, and experiment appropriately
             in reforming and implementing approved rites.
46 Likewise there are to be formed commissions
       on sacred music and sacred art,
             working in tandem and close cooperation
             with the liturgical commissions.

Chapter II:
The Most Sacred Mystery of the Eucharist

47 Jesus, the Christ, instituted the Eucharistic celebration
       at his last supper with his friends.
His purpose was a provide the Church

with a memorial of his loving death and resurrection:
> a sacrament of love
> a sign of unbreakable unity
> a bond of charity and justice,
>> all filling us with grace.

48 The Church earnestly wants the faithful, therefore,
> to find Jesus, the Christ present at the Eucharist.
The faithful should not be there
> as mere strangers or silent spectators,
> but are to take an active part in the rites
>> and understand what we're doing.

49 For this reason, we participants in Vatican II,
> having in mind mainly those Masses
>> where the faithful are present,
>> call for a revision of the rites
>> to make the liturgy more effective for all.

50 The rites of the Mass are, therefore, to be revised
> in such a way that their real purpose is served
> and the active participation of the faithful
>> will be increased.
The rites are to be simplified,
> duplications are to be eliminated
> and elements added with little advantage
>> are to be discarded.
Other elements which have suffered injury over time
> are to be restored to the vigor which they had
> during the days of the holy Fathers and Mothers,
>> or as may seem useful or necessary.

51 The treasures of the Bible are to be opened up
> and a more representative portion of them read
> so that a richer fare may be provided
>> at the table of God's word.

52 The homily should reflect on the mysteries of the faith,
> suggested by the rites or readings,
> and should not be omitted except rarely.

53 The prayer of the faithful following the homily
> is to be restored, and the people are to take part,
>> praying for the whole church,
>> the civil society,
>> and other needs.

54 The mother tongue may be used when suitable,
> especially for the readings and common prayers.

Whenever a more extensive use of the mother tongue
      is desirable, the regulations should follow article 40
         of this Constitution.
55 The faithful should receive communion at mass,
      and permission for communion under both kinds
      is granted at the discretion of the local bishops.
56 The two parts of the Mass:
      the liturgy of the word
         and that of the Eucharist are tightly linked
      and people should take part in the entire celebration.
57 Concelebration, where two or more priests or bishops
      celebrate with one another and the people,
      is to be restored for specific times and places
         as outlined in this article.
58 A new rite for concelebration should be drawn up.

Chapter III:
The other Sacraments and the Sacramentals

59 The purpose of the sacraments is to encourage holiness,
      to build up the Body of Jesus who is the Christ,
      and to give worship to God.
They are signs that also instruct.
      They presuppose faith but they also nourish,
         strengthen and express it.
They are sources of grace but also,
      the very act of celebrating them
      assists the faithful in receiving grace effectively.
Because they are so important,
      everyone should understand them well.

60 The Church has also instituted sacramentals,
      sacred signs which bear a resemblance to sacraments.
61 All this is meant to incorporate people's whole lives
      into the power of God.
62 But over time, there have crept into these sacred rites,
      certain features
         which have rendered their nature unclear.
We wish to reform them as well at this Council.

63 The mother tongue can be used more widely
      in celebrating the sacraments
      and can be of considerable help to people.

Following on article 36 of this Constitution
     the vernacular may be used when appropriate.
The rites are to be reformed and adapted to these times,
     taking into account the needs of different regions.
64 The catechumenate for adults is to be restored
     and appropriate rites developed
     to provide for initiation of the participants.
65 Elements of initiation rites already in use in mission lands
     are permitted when they can be suitably adapted
        for Christian use.
66 The rites for the baptism of adults is to be revised,
     taking into account its place in the catechumenate.
67 Likewise, the rites for the baptism of infants
     is to be revised,
     emphasizing more the role of parents and godparents.
68 These rites are to contain variants,
     to be used with local discretion,
     including some for use by catechists in mission lands.
69 A new rite is also to be devised for those already baptized
     celebrating their entry into full communion
        with the Catholic Church.
70 Except during Eastertide,
     baptismal water may be blessed
        within the rite of baptism,
        using a shorter formula.
71 Confirmation rites are to be revised
     with an emphasis on its connection to baptism;
     this rite should, in fact,
        include a renewal of baptismal promises.
     Confirmation may be celebrated within the Mass.
72 The rite and formula for the sacrament of penance
     is to be revised
     to better emphasize the nature of the sacrament
        with its focus on the mercy of God
73 "Extreme unction" will be called
     "anointing of the sick"
     and its rites and prayers are to be revised
     for use at times other than the point of death.
74 Those near death may be anointed
     before receiving communion.
75 Furthermore, the sick may be anointed more than once
     and the rite should reflect

the varying conditions of health.
76 The rites and texts for the ordination of priests
      are to be revised.
When a bishop is consecrated, all other bishops present
      shall participate in the laying of hands.
77 The rites for marriage are to be revised
      and may include suitable local customs.
In all cases, the priest must ask for and obtain
      the consent of the parties.
78 Matrimony should typically be celebrated
      within the Mass,
      with the prayer for the bride amended
      to remind both parties of their equal obligation
         to remain faithful to each other.
79 Sacramentals are to undergo a revision
      which takes into account the principle
      of active, intelligent participation by the faithful.
         Some may be administered by laypeople.
80 The rites for the consecration of virgins
      and for religious profession and renewal
      should be drawn up to achieve greater dignity.
Such a profession of vows should generally be made
      within the Mass.
81 The rite for the burial of the dead
      should express more clearly the connection
      to Jesus' death and rising
         and should take into account customs found
         in various regions.
82 Finally, the rite for the burial of children
      should be revised
      and a special Mass provided for the occasion.

Chapter IV:
The Divine Office

83 The work of Jesus is a song of praise for God
      and the Church now continues that hymn
         by celebrating the Eucharist
         but also by praying the divine office.
84 An ancient tradition of the Church,
      the divine office is composed in such a way
      that all the hours of day and night
         are filled with prayer.

This is the very prayer of the Body of Jesus!

85 Therefore, those who pray this holy office
      have the special honor
      of representing the whole Church
          standing before God in praise daily.
86 Prayer and the ministry of the word
      were tightly linked by the early followers of Jesus
      whose example we now take.
87 But in order to make this more powerful
      and a greater benefit to all who pray it,
      the Council wishes to enact certain reforms.
88 First and foremost, the prayer will be re-organized
      so that the prayers are genuinely related
          to the hour of the day
          at which they are prayed.
We will also take into account
      the modern conditions of apostolic ministry
      and how daily life is lived in these times.
89 We declare first, therefore,
      (a) that Lauds as morning prayer and
      Vespers as evening prayer
          are the two hinges on which the office turns.
          These are the chief hours
          and should be observed as such.

      (b) Compline will be revised as a suitable evening prayer
          for the end of the day.
      (c) The other hours of prayer will be revised as well.
          (d) Prime is to be suppressed
          and (e) Terce, Sext, and None are to be adjusted
          according to this article.
90 Those who pray the office
      should attune their minds and hearts to the prayer
      and revisions should make this more possible,
91 including revision of the readings,
      the hymns,
      the length of the psalter,
      and the time of day.
92 The readings in the divine office shall be revised
      to include a rich presentation of Scripture,
      excerpts from the Fathers,

and accounts of martyrdom that reflect actual facts.
93 Hymns should be revised to their original form
and all mythology and undesirable forms of piety
are to be removed.
94 The hours should be prayed at a time
which closely corresponds
with the intent of the prayer.
95 Communities are bound to celebrate the office daily
according to the norms of this article.
96 Clerics who do not live in community,
are required to pray the divine office alone
97 In certain cases, a liturgical service
may substitute for the office
or a person may be dispensed from praying it
all at the discretion of the local bishop.
98 Members of religious institutes whose constitutions
obligate them to pray specific parts of the office,
or to pray any short office
also take part in this public prayer.
99 Priests living in common who pray together,
are expressing the praise of the Church
when they pray.
When possible, the office should be sung.
100 Laypeople, too, are encouraged to pray the divine office
with local priests, among themselves,
or even individually.
101 Latin is to be retained for the office
but the local bishop may allow the mother tongue
when the use of Latin is an obstacle to understanding.

Chapter V:
The Liturgical Year

102 The Church unfolds its celebrations of the mysteries
of the faith in an annual calendar,
observing Sundays each week
as well as a cycle of feasts
from Christmas to Pentecost.
103 In so doing, we honor Mary with special devotion.
104 The memory of the martyrs and other saints
is also commemorated.
105 Likewise, the various seasons of traditional discipline
such as Advent and Lent

complete the formation of the faithful
and provide a time for acts of penance and mercy.

Therefore, this Council sees fit to declare:
106 Sunday is the original feast day
        and is a day when the faithful come together
                in one place.
The faithful should develop Sunday as a time of joy
        and freedom from work.
                In fact, Sunday and its liturgical celebration
                are to be a focus of Church life.
107 The calendar of the liturgical year is to be revised
        to suit modern times
        and nourish the faithful.
A clear focus on the paschal mystery of the Lord
        should always be clear.
108 The feasts of the Lord take precedence over all others.
Hence, the sacred seasons of Advent-Christmastide
        and Lent-Eastertide
        should be emphasized to nourish the faithful.
109 The season of Lent is both
        a time of preparation for baptism
        and a time of penance for the faithful.
Hence, elements of baptismal features should be restored
        as well as penitential elements.
In both cases, this season helps
        to prepare us for the Feast of Easter.
110 Hence, the practice of penance should be fostered
        in ways that suit our times and the local region.
111 We should continue to observe the feasts of the saints
        provided they do not overshadow feasts of the Lord
        and only feasts with a truly universal character
                should be observed in the universal Church.

Chapter VI:
Sacred Music
112 The Church has a great treasure in its music,
        more so than any other art,
        because sacred song united to the words
        forms a necessary part of the solemn liturgy.
Therefore, sacred music should conform and be drawn
        from the liturgical actions themselves.

Hence, this Council sets down these norms:

113 Liturgical worship is more noble when sung,
    especially the divine office.
114 Hence choirs must be promoted
    but all the faithful should also sing
    as part of the active participation
    we have called for here.
115 Music is to be taught in all seminaries
    and houses of formation.
116 While the church considers Gregorian Chant
    especially well-suited for the liturgy,
    it likewise admits other forms of music,
    especially polyphony.
117 An edition of a Gregorian Chant hymnal
    for use in smaller parishes should be prepared.
118 Singing by the people should be fostered
    to help everyone pray more enthusiastically.
119 Local musical traditions should be welcomed
    when suitable.
120 In the Roman Catholic Church the pipe organ
    is to be held in high esteem
    but other instruments may be used
    provided they are dignified and genuinely contribute
    to the edification of the faithful.
121 Composers should be encouraged
    and they should draw the words for their music
    principally from holy Scripture and liturgical sources.

Chapter VII:
Sacred Art and Furnishings

122 The church has a long tradition of appreciating
    and incorporating fine arts into its worship spaces
    because by their very nature,
        such works give praise to God.
The Church has always been a friend to the arts
    helping to decide which works give praise to God
    and which are fitting for sacred use.
Hence this Council sets down these norms:

123 As such, we admit all kinds of art,
    taking no one particular style as our own,

      provided that what is chosen
        is dignified and edifying.
124 And whether in selecting and retaining art
      or sacred vessels and vestments
      pastors should strive after noble beauty
        rather than sumptuous display.
Bishops should carefully remove any artworks
      which are repugnant to faith, morals, or piety.
When new churches are built, care should be taken
      that they are suitable for liturgical celebrations
      including the participation of the faithful.
125 Placing sacred images in churches may be continued
      but their number should be moderate
      and their relative placement in right order.
126 Bishops and pastors should consult
      their commission on sacred art
        when making selections.
127 Bishops should help to imbue artists
      with the spirit of the sacred
      and schools to support sacred art should be founded.
128 Along with the revisions of the liturgical books,
      there is to be an early revision of the statutes
      which govern material things involved with worship,
        including embellishments and vestments.
Local bishops are empowered
      to make most of these determinations.
129 Seminarians are to be taught about sacred art,
      its history and meaning,
      so they, too, will assist in its promotion.
130 It is fitting, finally, that bishops or others of such rank
      continue to wear signs of their ministry.

The Dogmatic Constitution on the Church
From the Second Vatican Council
Promulgated by Pope Paul VI on November 21, 1964
Lumen Gentium

Chapter I:
The Mystery of the Church

1 Christ is the Light of the nations.
Because this is so, we bishops of the world,
  gathered by the Holy Spirit
  at this Second Vatican Council,
  eagerly desire to bring this Light
    to people everywhere
    by making the gospel accessible
      to all of creation.
The Church is in Jesus, the Christ;
  it is a sacrament of Christ, a mystery of depth.
It is both a sign and an instrument
  of intimate union with God
  and of the total union of humans to one another.
And, therefore, the Church now wants
  to share with the whole world
  its own inner nature and mission.
This document does that.
In doing so, it remains faithful to previous councils
  while at the same time taking stock of these times.
Our world society is wonderfully united today
  by technology and culture.
But that alone is not enough to fulfill our human destiny.
  And, in fact, such secular unity
  only makes it all the more urgent
  that we should also come to full human unity
    in Jesus the Christ.

2 With most profound wisdom and goodness,
  God created the whole world
  and from among all of the creation
  God chose us, humans, to share in the divine life,
    to have an eternal walk with God,

arm in arm and heart to heart.
And although we have stumbled along
    and at times have even lost our way,
      God has not abandoned us.
Instead, God remained radically present,
    eventually expressing the depth of parental love
      through Jesus.

3 Jesus is the one around whom the Church gathers.
Since the very beginning of time,
    God has been preparing this Church to receive Jesus.
    both in the ancient covenant with the people of Israel
      as well as in this age of the Holy Spirit.
At the end of time, all of God's plans
    will finally be brought to completion.
Then the Church will be a gathering of all who believe
    in Jesus, who is the Christ
    and all who have ever sought goodness. Salvation!
By being joined to Jesus, all of us were made
    children of God,
    sons and daughters of the one who created us,
      united in Jesus.
Thus, the Reign of God on Earth was inaugurated.

By Jesus' obedience and love,
    our relationship with God was restored.
Thus, too, Jesus' realm here on earth,
    which is fully present but seldom recognized,
    grows brighter and more visible
      as God's power unfolds.
Celebrating Eucharist over and over
    allows this power to unfold in the world
    and brings about our salvation.
Celebrating Eucharist over and over
    forms the Body of Jesus, the Christ,
    a unity into which everyone on earth is welcomed,
    unity in Jesus, who is the Light of the World.
        Lumen Gentium!

4 And now in our own age,
    we have the Holy Spirit to guide us.
This Spirit is a fountain of living water

springing up to life eternal!
The Spirit guides the Church in truth
    and continually makes the Church more holy.
Working through the ordinary lives of us all,
    the Spirit gives the Church everything it needs
    both for leadership and service
        and thus, allows the Church
        to keep its youthful energy.
Praying through the hearts of the faithful
    and dwelling in us as in a temple,
    the Spirit unifies us all in love.
And therefore, we can say that we, the Church,
    are a people united by our common heritage:
        created in love by God,
        assembled in the name of Jesus,
        and bound together in the Holy Spirit.

5 We are at a loss to explain this beautiful divine mystery
    and to understand it fully
    no matter how long and faithfully we plumb it.
That's because it is a mystery of depth,
    not misunderstanding.
The Church itself is a mystery like this
    which can be understood, therefore,
    only by coming to know its very foundation: Jesus.
Begun by his preaching the Good News
    which had been promised for centuries,
    this Church was enlivened and illuminated
        by the words, the works, the miracles,
        the very person of Jesus.
To better understand the Church,
    we use symbols and metaphors
    which come from sacred Scripture.
The Word of God is a seed, for example,
    as we read in Mark 4,
    a seed planted by a farmer.
Those who hear the Word which became flesh in Jesus
    actually live in the Reign of God here and now,
    a seed sprouting in them and growing to its harvest.
Jesus had a clear mission:
    that we might all have that seed planted within us
    and develop the inner spiritual energy to let it grow.

Jesus, the Christ, showed us the way of self-giving love
  full of charity, humility, and self-sacrifice,
  and this is the way of the Kingdom of God.
The Church now takes up the work of Jesus the Christ,
  guided by the Holy Spirit,
  and continues to sow that seed of faith
    building up that Kingdom.

6 Using other metaphors and images,
  which are found within the Bible
  we describe the Church.
In one place, the Church is compared
  to a flock of sheep with its shepherd;
  in another, to a field being cultivated by the farmer;
  and in yet another, to a relationship between lovers
    budding into romance and passion.
Sometimes it is referred to as a vineyard
  where the vine delivers life-giving sap to each branch
    to nourish it and make it fruitful.
Other times, the Church is called a building
  with Jesus as the cornerstone.
  Here is where the household of God is found,
    the family united by its parents.
  Here is the temple where God dwells,
    the heartbeat of a heavenly city
    where each of us is a living stone
    together forming this dwelling place of God.
The Church is also called "our mother"
  united to Jesus in an intimate relationship.
And perhaps the most touching metaphor in Scripture
  is the one where Jesus is called our very spouse,
    ready to give us radical love,
    a love that surpasses everything we know.

7 But for us Catholics and for all people,
  the most central and clear message we have
  emerges from the metaphor
  where we come to understand
    that we are family.
We are indeed brothers and sisters,
  because of the life and death
    which Jesus offered on our behalf.

We are, in fact, the very Body of Jesus, the Christ!
>But what does this mean,
>>to call ourselves the "Body of Jesus the Christ?!"

First, it means that we are united to Jesus
>in a remarkable way because of baptism
>which forms us in Jesus' image.
In baptism, every aspect of our Lord's being—
>his life, his death, his resurrection—
>>takes root in us, body and soul.
And, secondly, in the Eucharist,
>that which was begun in baptism
>is nourished continuously and affirmed.
In the Eucharist, we experience real communion,
>genuine fellowship, and undeniable connectedness
>>with Jesus and with all people.
By these two sacraments, we become
>full members of the Church,
>and members of the Body of Jesus who is the Christ.
What we're actually saying here
>is that the Church *is* this Body.

Life in this Church is sometimes messy
>because the Church includes everyone
>with all their various talents and desires.
We would end up in a mess with all this
>if we did not have Jesus to lead us.

How does this work?
>How does Jesus lead the Church?
>The answer is both simple and complex,
>>and a large part of this document deals with it.
Jesus the Christ wants us to love each other,
>to endure sorrow with one another,
>to share happiness and to forgive each other freely,
>>all in a family-like lifestyle.
Therefore, whoever leads us as the Church
>toward a community filled with love,
>more significant and real love
>>lived out in everyday life,
>>that person speaks for Jesus.
That person is leading the Church in the name of Jesus.

There are many such leaders,
        each with his or her own diverse function.
Many people have gifts for leadership
        and offer them to the Church.
As Catholics, we believe that all this love,
        all these talents and desires
        are given "holy order" and made effective
                through the unity we have
                under the authority of the pope and bishops.
The presence of all these gifts,
        unified and directed by the Church
        forms the way in which Jesus and the Holy Spirit
                lead the Church
                and give it everything it needs
                to serve the world today.
Thus, Jesus the Christ leads the Church as its head,
        and the Holy Spirit sustains the Church
                as its soul.
We, then, as members of this Body
        must be conformed to the image of Jesus the Christ
        and the Holy Spirit of God.
We must be directed by our head, Jesus Christ,
        and by our soul, the Holy Spirit.
In this way, we serve one another unto salvation,
        which means that by loving each other
                we give each other the opportunity
                to be embraced by God
                and live with God eternally.

8 Given all this, we can clearly see now that Jesus both
        established and sustains the Church among us
                which is a community of faith, hope, and love.
We do not distinguish between the Body of Jesus the Christ
        which we have just described
        and the organized Church
                with its structures and leaders.
This is complex but can be understood this way:
        there is in the Church
        both a human and a divine element.
It is like Jesus' own nature, which is both human and divine.
This divine and human nature of the Church,
        where mystery and plainness swim together,

where the social structures swim
 with the Spirit of God,
  is the one Church of Jesus who is the Christ.
It is indeed one, and it is also holy, universal, and apostolic.
Part of the social structure given this Church by Jesus
 is the leadership of Peter
 who was commissioned as a shepherd,
 along with the other apostles,
 whose jobs were to help maintain this delicate truth
  that the Church is indeed the Body of Jesus.
And while this Church, organized in the world as a society,
 is found in the Catholic Church,
  many elements of truth and holiness
  are also found outside its structures.
These elements outside the Catholic Church
 are part of what urges us to desire greater unity
  among Christians.

We who claim to be the Church,
 we who claim to be the Body of Jesus the Christ,
 must resemble Christ as much as possible.
We must take the part of the poor whenever we can;
 we must defend those without power;
 we must avoid seeking our own glory
  and act with humility and self-sacrifice
  for the good of all.
We who are Christian
 and, indeed, the organized Church itself,
 must take in those who are afflicted,
  forgotten,
  and suffering.
The Church itself, like its members,
 is always in need of being renewed and forgiven,
  of being purified for its mission
  which is the same as the mission of Jesus.
And if we are faithful in this way as an organized Church
 and as its individual members,
 we will succeed in announcing Jesus to the world
  until all is seen in full light.
  Lumen Gentium!

Chapter II:
On the People of God

9 God has always welcomed anyone
      whose heart is ready to experience
      the divine presence.
These are the ones whose lives reflect goodness
      and who cultivate a sense of awe.
But God has also always chosen
      to welcome women and men,
      not merely as individuals
         but bound together,
         united as a people who recognize the divine.
So, coming together as a people
      is an essential element of salvation.
Hence, the house of Israel came as one people,
      united in a covenant with God,
      slowly growing more and more ready
         to receive God fully,
         ready to live within a full and new covenant.
In Jesus the Christ, this new covenant was instituted,
      and all were called together as a people:
         both Jew and Gentile,
         united in one common Spirit.
This would be "a chosen race,"
      as the First Letter of Peter calls it,
      "a royal priesthood, a holy nation, the people of God."
This people, which we call the Church,
      has Jesus as its head, as we have said already.
This people have the dignity and freedom
      of the sons and daughters of God.
      Its law is the commandment to love
         as Jesus, the great lover, loves us.
Its end is the Reign of God begun now here on earth
      and set to last for eternity.
Not all people belong to this Church,
      yet all people are included in the reach of its embrace.
The challenges and tasks which face the Church
      appear overwhelming at times.
Nonetheless, we are like a seed which will eventually
      bear the fruit of unity, hope, and healing for all.
The Church is continuously moving and searching,
      Wandering.

not unlike the Hebrew experience in the desert.
And even though the Church's movement
        is sometimes filled with trial and tribulation,
        nonetheless, it remains faithful overall.
It continues to be a visible sign of unity,
        a sacrament of salvation for all people.

Aware of the absolute importance of its mission,
        the Church seeks constant renewal.
It never ceases to beg the Holy Spirit for the grace it needs
        to be the Light of the World.

10 The baptized members of the Church,
        because they are consecrated by the Holy Spirit,
        share in the priesthood of Jesus Christ.
In the broadest sense,
        a priest is anyone
        who makes the world and its people holy
        by sacrificing and praying on its behalf.
In this sense, every single baptized person is a priest.
As priests, therefore, all the faithful are called
        to offer themselves to God
        and to offer the hope of God
                to one another.
They should, therefore, be faithful in prayer
        and live as part of the household of God.

We make a distinction, however,
        between the priesthood of the baptized
        and the priesthood of those ordained for ministry.
The ordained priest is charged to shape and bring holy order
        to the whole priestly people of God.
His ministry is to teach and serve all people.
Precisely because he is the one
        whose job is to give the Church order,
        he acts in the person and the power of Jesus the Christ
                when he presides at Eucharist.
Those in the baptized priesthood
        also join in offering the Eucharist.
They, too, serve in a priestly way
        by participating in the sacraments,
        by praying and offering thanks to God,

and by graciously serving their sisters and brothers.

11 In fact, the ideals of this priestly community
        become a reality when the members
                celebrate the sacraments
                and exercise habits of goodness.
Baptism and confirmation identify Christians
        as daughters and sons of God,
        willing to give their lives to the Church
        that others might experience the friendship of Jesus.
Eucharist provides them
        with the most profound source of strength
        and the highest moment of spiritual insight.
Reconciliation helps them focus on the mercy of God.
The sacred anointing of the sick
        lightens the load of suffering which they bear.
Those called to holy orders
        are appointed to feed the Church in Jesus' name
        with the Word and the grace of God.
And those called to matrimony
        live especially close to the unity and fruitful love
        which exists between Jesus Christ and the Church.
In fact, those who receive this sacrament,
        by reason of their state and rank in life,
        have their own unique gift among the People of God.
From their lovemaking comes forth
        new citizens of the world,
        those who will also ultimately live in the light.
This family setting is its own kind of Church,
        a sort of "domestic" Church.
In this household setting,
        where relationships are the stuff of daily life,
        for better or for worse, in sickness and in health,
                members witness to each other
                and teach each other to listen to the Spirit
                        prompting them in their hearts.
Hence, made strong by the power of God
        all the faithful regardless of their state of life
        are called to holiness by God himself.

12 When this whole Church,
        anointed as it is by the Holy Spirit,

believes together,
the truth of the Faith is absolutely undeniable.
It is like a chalice overflowing with so much truth
that even when everyone drinks from it,
it becomes fuller rather than emptier.
Such belief is ratified and declared through the leaders,
making everyone able to believe together.
This faith becomes clearer and more meaningful.
It becomes more believable to others
when believers practice it
in every aspect of their daily lives.
This same Spirit likewise sanctifies the whole world,
which means that through the Spirit
every aspect of the world will eventually be brought
to goodness and holiness.
This will happen because the Spirit gives gifts
to each person and assists each in using them well.
The power we need to do this comes only from God
and leads us insistently to more and more
become exactly who we are created to be.
We call this shared, loving, sacred power
by a name: we call it "grace."
Grace is "the energy of God in our lives,"
the loving presence of the divine one,
and it is given to everyone
at every rank of the Church.
It forms us into a community which also has a name:
The People of God!

13 All people everywhere and throughout all time
are called to belong to this People of God.
And does not this fit God's way of doing things?
God did, after all, create us in the divine image
to share human nature together.
Together we share an inescapable sameness.
God even became one of us in Jesus Christ
so that we might be united as human beings,
that we might begin to realize
that this sameness is a beautiful gift.
But human unity may seem like a far-off dream.
Our experience of national tensions
and cultural warfare

makes such worldwide unity appear impossible!
God's Reign, however, is not like an earthly one
          because it encompasses citizens of every race
                    with all their various cultures
                    and it forms these people into a Church.
In accepting these gifts of every nation,
          both spiritual and temporal,
          and uniting them into the one Family of God,
          the Church does not diminish the welfare of anyone.
On the contrary, it seeks to increase good everywhere.
Hence, we call the Church "catholic."
          a Greek word that means "universal."
          This means that all parts contribute to all others
                    and share their gifts in common.
Everyone is called, and everyone is related to this Church
          even though in a variety of ways.

14 For those called to be Catholic,
          the Church is necessary for salvation,
          according to both Scripture and Tradition.
We believe that for the Catholic faithful
          the Church is necessary for salvation
          because it is in the Church that we encounter Christ
                    who is "the Way."
Any Catholic who knows this
          and freely chooses to reject or leave the Church
          may ultimately also be choosing to reject salvation.
Not only that, being fully part of the Church means that we
          embrace all the Church has to offer:
                    creed, sacraments, community, and authority.
Beyond that, we must also live in love.
          The failure to put love into practice,
          even if we are faithful to the Church in all other ways,
                    is a rejection of salvation itself.
Those called to be catechumens are embraced as family
          as soon as the Holy Spirit stirs up in them
          the desire and will for full participation
                    in the life of the Church.

15 Those called to be Christians in other churches
          and with whom the pope is not yet fully united
          are nonetheless linked to the Church in many ways.

They are united to Catholics by Scripture,
       zeal for the teachings of Christ,
       belief in God as creator, and prayer.
Many others celebrate the Eucharist
       honor Mary as the mother of Jesus,
       practice works of charity and mercy,
       and live in the light of the Spirit.
Together we hope and work toward full unity.
The Church urges all its members to lives
       that are holy and renewed to enable this.

16 And, finally, the many people who are not Christian
       are also connected to the People of God.
The Jews remain dear to God, for example,
       as do the people of Islam,
              as well as all those who seek God
              with a sincere heart.
Likewise, those who seek no God whatsoever,
       if they are good and true,
       are also related to God's people.
Only those who persist in darkness and cultivate despair
       have cut off their relationship
       to the People of God.

17 Following the desire and command of Jesus,
       the Church makes a serious effort
       to present the gospel to the whole world
              so that people can share in God's love.
Everyone who is baptized is charged with this mission.

The Church works and prays diligently
       with great hope that everyone in the whole world
       will ultimately join together as the People of God.

Chapter III:
On the hierarchical structure of the Church,
in particular the bishops

18 As we have said, Jesus instituted a variety of ministries
       within the Church for the good of the whole Body.
Among these is the role of bishop,
       which flows from the relationship
       of Jesus to his closest apostles,

and especially with Peter as their leader.
We believe that Christ wants these leaders
>and their successors
>>to continue in their roles for all time.
And we also want to lay out plainly here
>what the role of the bishop is
>and how bishops work with each other
>>and with the pope
>>>to guide and direct the household of God.

19 Jesus prayerfully called an initial twelve apostles
>whose sole desire
>was to spend their lives in his presence.
Thus, Jesus formed a permanent community of leadership
>a sort of "college" with them.
They were eventually sent out to teach, preach, heal,
>and minister to the people of that age.
They were sent to spread the Faith to all the world.
And they were confirmed in this mission
>by the Holy Spirit at Pentecost,
>as Acts of the Apostles tells us.
Eventually, they came to be called "bishops."

20 These first ones appointed by Jesus who is the Christ
>soon added others and down through history
>such appointments have continued
>so that since the time of Jesus
>there has been a steady succession of bishops,
>passing on the mantel of ministry and leadership
>>and continuing the work of Jesus.
With priests and deacons to help them,
>the bishops preside over the People of God,
>taking the place of the apostles in doing so.
Whoever listens to them is listening to Jesus.

21 The authority which bishops exercise requires wisdom,
>understanding, and sincerity of heart.
These gifts are given to a bishop in his ordination
>and become operative
>as he puts them into practice.
The primary role of the bishop
>is to be a shepherd for God's people,

helping them to maintain a sense of order,
             harmony, and unity.
To do this, bishops receive a unique outpouring
             of the Holy Spirit passed to them
             through the laying on of hands
                   at the time of their consecration.
This gives them "the fullness of the priesthood,"
             meaning they are named as those
             who take the place of Jesus for us.
And it follows then that these bishops
             sharing in the ministry of the pope,
             can confer the sacrament of holy orders.

22 Bishops are not free agents;
             they are bound together as a college,
             speaking in unity with the pope,
                   in a bond of charity and peace.
Together with the pope,
             who is the successor of Peter and the bishop of Rome,
             the bishops are called to reflect
                   perfect unity among themselves.
Maintaining this unity of faith and unity of heart
             among Catholic people
             is a crucial aspect of the Church.
This Second Vatican Council reaffirms this
             by clearly enunciating the importance
             of the role of the bishops
             and their relation to the pope.
As such, the gathering of this very council
             expresses a model of operating for the Church.
 In this model, the opinion of the many
             is prudently considered
             when making decisions about important matters.
We have a long history of holding councils such as this one
             where we consider major questions together.
An ecumenical council, however,
             has no authority unless it speaks in one voice
             with the bishop of Rome.
It is infallible if and only if it teaches in unity with the pope.
Ultimately, the bishop of Rome
             has authority over all bishops,
             and is pastor of the universal church.

23 The pope is the visible foundation of unity
        for the whole Church.
Individual bishops likewise serve as a sign of unity
        in their own dioceses where they work
In their role, bishops must help maintain this universal unity
        and guide the faithful to love the Body of Christ
                especially those who are poor or sorrowing.
They are also concerned
        with the welfare of the whole Church.
        And this universal unity also extends
                to other churches
        established over time
        with their own liturgical traditions,
                church law, and spiritual heritage.

24 The ministry of the bishop is one of service
        to those among whom he stands.
25 In the local diocese,
        the bishop is the authentic teacher of faith and morals,
        and the faithful are to accept his teaching.
Toward this end,
        preaching the gospel holds the first priority.
        Bishops preach and teach this way,
        in union with the pope
                and under his watchful concern.
They do not enjoy the prerogative of infallibility
        but when they are in union with the pope
        they teach the authentic faith,
                especially when they teach through a council.

26 Bishops are responsible for seeing to it
        that the people in the dioceses they serve
        have the opportunity to celebrate the sacraments,
                especially the Eucharist.
The Church is fully present in all local groups of the faithful
        when the group is organized legitimately
                and united to its pastor.
Jesus is fully present in each of these "altar communities"
        because Jesus is present
        whenever the Eucharist is celebrated.
Each local community, therefore,
        is a microcosm of the whole Church,

fully reflecting the goodness of God
and suffering the difficulties of everyday life.
Hence, among the official duties of bishops
are the tasks of caring for the poor and lonely
and assisting other dioceses in need of help.
Bishops pray and toil for the people,
and through the sacraments, they give the faithful
everything needed to attain salvation.

27 By their manner of life,
their advice to the faithful,
and their exhortations,
bishops lead their people.
Theirs is a humbling power meant only to lead others
to spiritual development.
They are not vicars of the pope
but vicars of Jesus Christ himself!
Their model, therefore, is that of the Good Shepherd,
who came to serve and not be served,
who came to lay down his life for his flock!
For their part, the faithful should be kindly disposed
toward their bishops!

28 It would be humanly impossible for any bishop
to do everything needed in the Church.
Therefore, God has established
three levels of ordained ministry:
bishop, priest, and deacon.
Priests participate in the ministry of the bishop.
They are consecrated to preach the gospel,
shepherd the faithful in unity,
and celebrate divine worship.
Their most visible and vital role
is that of presiding at Eucharist.
In this ministry, they are most tightly connected to
the person of Christ and the mission of their bishop.
They labor in word and doctrine,
believing what they read and meditating on that,
teaching what they believe,
and putting into practice in their own lives
what they teach.
Working with their bishops,

priests strive to lend their effort to the pastoral work
of the whole diocese and even of the entire Church.
They share an intimate brotherhood with each other,
offering one another mutual aid,
spiritual and material,
pastoral and personal.
Priests are to look after the spiritual needs
of the parishes entrusted to them
with the concern of a caring father
who tends his family with love.
Through their daily conduct and care,
they have a genuinely priestly and pastoral ministry
both to believers and nonbelievers
to Catholics and non-Catholics.

29 In the very early years of the Church,
deacons, too, participated
in the ministry of their bishop.
However, over the centuries
the diaconate has fallen into disuse.
Because of the needs of the world,
this council now gives approval
to the restoration of the diaconate.
Deacons have a ministry of service
to administer solemn baptism,
dispense the Eucharist,
witness marriages,
bring viaticum to the dying,
read the Scriptures to the faithful,
administer sacramentals,
officiate at funerals,
and be dedicated to charity and administration.
Under the rules of the restored diaconate,
even married men can be ordained deacon.
But if an unmarried man is ordained,
he must remain celibate forever.

Chapter IV:
The Laity

30 It is clear that bringing order to the Church
and keeping us all moving together on the right path
requires a well-ordered system.

The Dogmatic Constitution on the Church   161

Toward this end, members of the hierarchy—
    bishops, priests, and deacons—
        have a clearly defined and quite specific role
            within the Church.
Less defined, but equally important, is the role
    of those called to be members of the laity.
This Second Vatican Council now eagerly outlines
    the indispensable role of the layperson.

31 When we speak of "the laity,"
    we include all the baptized members of the Church
    except sisters, brothers, and clergy.
32 The Church is full of diversity, as Jesus wanted.
    We are one body with many members,
    each member having gifts which are to be used
        for the good of all.
All members of the Church share true equality
    with regard to their dignity and their calling.
There is in Jesus who is the Christ
    complete equality regardless of race,
        nationality,
        social condition,
        and gender.
Everyone has a distinct role to play,
    and all roles work together to build up the Church.
Hence, pastors should minister to each other and the people
    and the people should lend assistance to their pastors.
Jesus is our brother
    and he came to serve, not to be served
    which is how the Church is also organized.

33 Lay ministry is a participation
    in the mission of the Church,
    not merely an aid to the work of the clergy.
Through baptism, all are called and gifted
    and from the Eucharist all are sent to love and serve.
There are some matters which pertain specifically
    to laywomen and men,
    but everything said above about the People of God
        applies equally to everyone in the Church.
The pastors of the Church
    know how much the laity contributes

to the welfare of the Church and of the world.
They must not force every aspect of the Church
upon the rest of the world
nor can they neglect the wisdom and goodness
that the Church can offer to society.
Every layperson is, therefore,
at the same time a witness
and a living instrument of the mission
of the Church itself.
The laity receive from Christ and from the Church
everything that is necessary to fulfill their vocation.

34 As the role of the ordained priest
is to consecrate bread and wine
to be the Body and Blood of Jesus the Christ
so the role of the layperson
is to consecrate the entire world.
Lay people live in ordinary circumstances
of family and social life
which is where they are called by God.
By their lifestyles—
their work,
their prayer,
their family life,
their leisure and entertainment,
and their hardships too—
laypeople give witness
to the Light of Jesus, who is the Christ.
35 The laity go forth as powerful proclaimers
of a Faith in things to be hoped for.
Lay people share in the one priesthood of Jesus Christ.
The Gospel shines forth in their daily lives,
in their family and social lives,
and in all their secular activities.
From Jesus, they receive an authentic sense of faith,
an inner voice
which sounds the call of truth,
and the Word of God
which directs this truth.
Marriage and family life are a holy state through which,
by the power of the Holy Spirit,
the world is made holy.

The Christian family loudly proclaims God's love.
Let the laity devote themselves to a profound grasp
      of the teachings of the Church
      and let them be imbued with the wisdom of God.

36 While the ordained person concerns himself
      with bringing "holy order" to the Church,
      the layperson is concerned with
      bringing "holy order" to the world.
The task of the laity is to animate the world
      with the Spirit of Jesus who is the Christ,
          tending the poor,
          establishing justice for all,
      and illuminating the world with the light of Christ.
Thus, the laity are entrusted with the critical job
      of ordering the world's goods
      so that all people are cared for
          and no one is overlooked.
It is up to the lay people to oversee
      the customs and conditions of the world.
      Let them order these according to the norms
          of justice,
          peace,
          and the dignity of all.
All Christians, especially those
      who share the special sacrament of married life,
      loudly proclaim this Faith:
          the presence of the Reign of God,
          the hope of blessings to come.
In doing so, they must wrestle and stand against
      all in this world
          that is not of God.
It is the responsibility of laypeople
      to maintain the delicate and subtle balance
      between Church and society.

37 Thus, the vocation of each layperson
      is to seek the Reign of God
      in his or her everyday work
          and to direct that work
          according to God.
Lay people have the obligation

to continually develop a more profound grasp
of their Christian faith.
Lay people also receive
spiritual goods from the Church
and from their pastors.
Since they need these spiritual goods to fulfill their call,
such goods are not only a privilege,
but a right as well.
In order to receive what they really need,
they must express their needs and wants openly.
They must be attentive to the direction of the Church
and play a part in providing leadership.
There are even times
when laypeople have a serious obligation
to express their opinions and insights
about the Church.
Their wisdom and knowledge
often arise from valuable life experience.
Such wisdom is to be prized by Church leaders.
When laypeople challenge the Church
it should be through official channels
and with courage,
respect,
and above all, charity.
In the end, laypeople should embrace
as fully as possible,
what their pastors decide.

It is imperative that laypeople
pray for their pastors.
Pastors must likewise pray for their parishioners,
trust their wisdom,
and take to heart all they have to say.
They should be open
to all the different talents, gifts, and experiences
that laypeople bring to the Church.
Pastors must give real responsibility to parishioners
and encourage them
to take the initiative in their parishes.
Such authentic trust and cooperation
between the laity and their spiritual leaders
holds excellent potential for the Church:

Lay people will take greater ownership in the Church
    and gain renewed enthusiasm
        for wholehearted cooperation
            with their pastors.
The ordained will likewise be better equipped
        to make wise decisions
            regarding both spiritual and temporal matters.
38 In the end,
        the Christian layperson must be to the world
        what the soul is to the body.

Chapter V:
The Universal Call to Holiness in the Church

39 The Church is holy.
        The Church was holy.
            The Church will always be holy.
We know this to be true because
        Jesus loves the Church into holiness
        and gives her the presence of the Holy Spirit.
This holiness is made evident
        by the many women and men
        who draw from the Church
            the Spirit and strength
            to live lives of holy goodness.
40 We are called to holiness by Christ himself
        who taught, in the words of Matthew,
        that we must be "perfect as God is perfect."
By transforming the activities and events
        of everyday life into holy moments,
        all the faithful grow in this perfection
        and the world more and more resembles God's Reign.
So it is clear that everyone —
        lay, religious, and ordained —
        is called to be holy.

"Love God with all your heart," the Scriptures tell us,
        "with all your soul, with all your understanding,
            and with all your strength.
            Love one another as Christ loves you."
These commands in Scripture
        are really an invitation to be holy.
By our holy love, we nurture in the world

a way of life that is gentler,
    beautiful,
    and humane.
Over and over again, the Scriptures describe for us
    what this holiness will resemble:
            a heart of mercy, humility, meekness,
            patience, awareness of God's mercy
            when we have sinned,
            and a spirit of forgiveness toward others.

41 There are many ways to live out this call to be holy.
Everyone should walk
        according to his or her own personal gifts and duties,
            in the pathway of a living faith.
Bishops are to be so faithful to this call
        that they would lay down their lives
        for the people that they serve.
Priests have a particular duty
        to make prayer an integral part of their daily lives,
                thus making their service more authentic
                and their sacrifice more genuine.
Deacons and other people called to Church ministry
        should model their lives after the apostles
        who worked tirelessly for the gospel.
Married couples and parents
        should sustain one another in grace
        throughout the entire length of their lives.
Widows and single people likewise
        give witness to their holiness
        through their labors in the Church in society.
For those called to them,
        the promises of chastity, obedience, and poverty
        are also a means to holiness.
Others, particularly those who suffer,
        from poverty, infirmity, and illness,
        those who bear injustice and hardship
        also find holiness in their unique relationship
                with Jesus, who suffered.
42 Love is the principal way to holiness.
Beyond that and included within it are other pathways:
        the sacraments, especially the Eucharist,
        self-sacrifice, prayer, service to others,

and virtue lived every day.
Therefore, all the faithful of Jesus the Christ
    are invited to strive for holiness,
        even perfection.
This call takes the form that Jesus showed us:
        to practice self-giving love as he did on the cross,
            and to be obedient to our conscience
            that is, obedient to what God is asking of us.
Let all hear God's call within them,
    each one observant and appreciative
    of life's unique treasures.
Let neither the use of the things of this world
    nor attachment to riches
    hinder them in their quest for perfect love.

Chapter VI:
Religious

43 Another way in which many women and men
    choose to live out their baptismal call
        is to be part of a religious order.
In doing so, they embrace the "evangelical counsels."
    That is, they take vows
        of poverty,
        chastity,
        and obedience.
Indeed, this is a "Gospel way of life,"
    for it is founded on the teaching and example
        of Christ.

Throughout its history,
    the Church has affirmed the evangelical counsels
    and recognized them as a profound gift.
The Church desires to promote this way of life
    and keep it safe from whatever would harm it,
    either from the outside or from within.
Therefore, the Church is concerned
    about those called to this way of life.
It assists them in forming lasting commitments
    to their communities
    and in keeping the ideals of poverty,
        chastity,
        and obedience

in their proper perspective.
There are many forms of religious life.

Some live in community while others live in solitude.
There are religious orders of sisters, brothers, laypeople,
  and priests.
All of them seek to embody the ideals of their founders
  and the Spirit of Jesus, who is the Christ.
The religious state of life is not an intermediate state
  between ordination and lay life.
Instead, it holds a place of its own in the Church
  and includes members of both clergy and laity.

44 A person enters the religious life
  by way of vows or promises,
  eventually committing her or himself for life.
Indeed, in baptism, everyone is called
  to live a life of holiness.
  These vows help an individual
  to put this baptismal call into practice.
Those who make such vows in religious life
  consecrate their entire lives to God
  in a particular and public way.
In this form of radical Christian life,
  they have the freedom to serve God and the Church
  wherever they are needed most.

45 Religious orders are approved and promoted
  by the local bishop,
  thus assuring that there will be genuine cooperation
  between the various ministries that exist in a diocese.
46 They have a duty to work diligently
  to implant and strengthen the Reign of God
   in our times.
This can happen both through prayer
  and active apostolic labor.
Those living consecrated lives should remember well
  that both believer and nonbeliever
  find Christ in them daily.
In a concrete way, they demonstrate to the world
  how Jesus prayed privately on the mountain,
  proclaimed the Reign of God to the crowds,

healed the sick,
worked to lead all to a better life,
and lived in obedience to the One who sent him.
47 So let all the faithful realize
that by committing themselves to these vows,
women and men religious do not alienate themselves
from other people or from the world.
Nor do they become useless members of our human society.
For even they who do not live and mingle
among their contemporaries
still maintain a strong spiritual bond
with all other Christians.
This council encourages and praises
those who generously offer themselves in service
as religious sisters and brothers.

Chapter VII:
The Pilgrim Church and the Communion of Saints

48 We are called to be together in the Church
and, through God's grace, to achieve holiness.
But we are not yet fully holy, loving, and forgiving,
and we must continue to grow in holiness
all the days of our lives
as we deepen our connection to Jesus.
The People of God experienced
the life-giving Spirit of Christ
in a profound way after the Resurrection.
And even though Jesus the Christ
is now invisible to us as a person
he remains active among us in the Church
and present to us in his very body and blood.

God is love, and we are the objects of God's love.
Jesus has already made us aware of these close ties to God
and invited us to live in that kingdom.
In the Church as we celebrate the sacraments,
live in community, and serve one another,
we learn the true meaning of our lives.
Through faith, we come to understand
our unique role in bringing
about this awareness of love
by helping the world reflect God's goodness.

There is cause for great excitement here.
This new way of love and forgiveness has already begun,
    indeed, is already here
    and we are invited to be part of it.
There is also a tension which we can clearly recognize:
    We know we are children of God's love
        because we have experienced it
        in beauty, relationships, and community.
Yet we still live with all the pain and difficulty
    of being unable to see this clearly.
    Fear, anger, and aggression remain with us.
We are, indeed, sons and daughters of God
    while at the same time
        we are often unaware of God's presence
        and we wait for even fuller union with God.

God's love for us is so great and mysterious
    that we can glimpse only a little of it now.
Even the little we now see, however, is really awesome!
We believe that God's love is always waiting for us
    to receive it,
    like water hidden by a dam,
        a reservoir of love is poised
        to flow out upon those who love.
And one day we hope to see and feel this divine love
    in all its force and power.
So we should live in readiness and expectation
    as though that might occur today
    because none of us knows for sure when it will come.

The Scriptures are filled with images of this Reign of God
    and the day when God's love will be fulfilled.
We know that at some point, a judgment will be made
    about how we have chosen to live
    and those who are strangers to God's love,
    who have held an umbrella of hate all their lives,
    will be unable to see and experience God's love.
Those who recognize God,
    who have stood out in the Reign of God
    loving and serving one another,
    will gladly welcome God's abundant presence.

They will live in eternal goodness.

49 At the present time, while all await God's full return,
    some of us among the faithful live our lives now,
    some have died and are moving toward the light,
    and others live in intimate union with God.
But all of us are in one great communion,
    bound together in God's love
    which is unbroken by death.
Those who have died live fully with God,
    yet they remain united to us in love.
            They now serve God closely
            and know God completely.
Thus, they add a dimension of holiness to the Church:
    They pray for us.
    They worship with us.
    They lend us their spiritual strength in our weakness.

50 Therefore, it is right and fitting
    for us to cultivate the memory of the dead:
    including of course Mary, the saints,
            and other holy ones,
    our own loved ones and those who taught us.
We remember those who have died
    because their lives inspire us
    to maintain hope in all that God has in store for us.
By following in their footsteps,
    we arrive at perfect union with Christ:
    we arrive, in a word, at "holiness."

Our ongoing union with our beloved dead
    is most powerful when we celebrate the liturgy.
In the Eucharist, the whole communion of Christ,
    living and dead, gathers around the table.
At that moment, we are truly one great Church:
    the whole Body of Christ
            present in mystery and friendship.
And here is a critical point in all of this:
    We who live and pray during our lifetimes
    are not united with a "different" Christ
    than those who live and pray in heaven!
No, there is one Christ, one Lord, who unites us all in love.

Truly the Eucharist is a marvelous gathering
of all the faithful, living and dead!

51 This council affirms the ancient teachings of the Church
regarding our relationship to those who have died
and their essential place in the Church.
But we also recognize that certain abuses have crept in
and urge that they be corrected.
Our veneration of the saints,
our fondness for those who have died,
is not about miracles and other external acts.
It is about intensifying our practice of love.
Hence, a genuine and authentic remembering of the dead
will enhance our worship and bring us closer to God.

Chapter VIII:
The Blessed Virgin Mary in the Mystery of Christ
& the Church

52 God is ultimately wise and good
and knows humankind intimately.
Before we speak, God knows the desires of our souls
and how they are best fulfilled.
That is why God was revealed so fully in Jesus the Christ,
the Light of the World
who also taught that we, too, are such a light.
Like Jesus, we are also fully with God
and, at the same time, fully human.

Jesus did not appear among us as if by magic.
Instead, Jesus is a reflection of God's inner self
and God's relationship to humankind.
Jesus' presence showed us the way to freedom,
to genuine and permanent commitment,
and to divine intimacy.
Because of this, the Mother of Jesus was someone
who was also entirely free,
committed to faith,
and filled with God's love and grace.
God called Mary, and Mary said yes to God.

53 Because of this, we as Christians
can never take for granted

the gift that Mary presented to us
        and nurtured for us:
        the gift of divine love, Jesus who is the Christ.
For this, we respect, revere, and honor Mary.
54 This council wants to make clear
        what we as Catholics believe about Mary.
        We want to describe her role in the Incarnation,
        and we want to describe
                how we can best respond to Mary.
In short, we want to nurture
        a healthy relationship with Mary
        by coming to understand her proper role
                in our salvation.

55 Mary is acknowledged as both the Mother of God
        and Mother of the Redeemer.
Because of this, she has a place of honor
        both in the Church and in heaven.
She has a unique relationship to God
        and a special relationship to the Church.
And although she is unlike us in these ways,
        she is also *like* us in the most fundamental aspects
                of her nature:
She, too, is in need of salvation simply
        because she is human.
Mary does not stand above Jesus,
        but stands with all of us who need spiritual freedom.
What a remarkable relationship this is!
        Jesus depended on Mary for the things of this earth.
        Mary depended on Jesus for the things of heaven!
This, of course, means that Mary is a member of the Church
        and an excellent example of faith and charity.
We Catholics, therefore, honor her with childlike affection.

From the very beginning of time,
        God had something extraordinary planned for Mary.
The place of Mary in the plan of salvation
        is even foretold in the writings of Isaiah:
                "A virgin shall give birth to a son
                and the nations will call him Emmanuel."
        That name, Emmanuel, means "God with us."
        And indeed, Jesus' message was precisely that:

The reign of God is among us.
We seek God within.
Yet though she was part of God's plan,
Mary was free to say yes or no to God.
Her role was not forced upon her.

56 Rather, God had great things in store for Mary,
and she freely chose to accept them.
That willingness on her part to serve
is an essential part of the working out of holiness,
the fight against sin in the world,
and the coming of the Holy Spirit.
It is no wonder that the earliest members of the Church
quickly developed a sense of awe
at Mary's place and role!
Mary was full of grace, an offer which is also made to us.

This is often seen as the reversal
of the story of Adam and Eve,
where, in figurative language,
we come to understand that only by love
can we survive.
And love is found only in obedience
to what God is asking of us,
which Mary offered freely
and which we are also called upon to offer God.
Hence through Mary and Joseph,
a new way to human fulfillment was opened,
a new pathway that was of self-giving love.

57 We see this new pathway to love revealed
in how Elizabeth greeted Mary
and called her "blessed,"
causing the infant to leap within her.
We see it again when Jesus was presented in the temple,
amid the prophetic words of Simeon.
And yet again we see it in the story of Jesus being lost
and after three days, found.
All of these were part of Mary's parental devotion and work,
and all of them complete the unfolding story
of the Incarnation.
58 Indeed, in Jesus' ministry,

Mary was also present at critical moments.
From Cana to the Cross, Mary was present:
    faithful mother,
    faithful daughter of God.
59 After Jesus' death, Mary remained present:
    she persevered in prayer and waited in faith
        with the apostles and the other women
        who had also known Jesus.
And we believe Mary is now as close to Jesus as ever,
    present with God in heaven.

60 Jesus is the one Mediator between God and humanity.
Because of the Holy Spirit,
    we have a direct friendship with Jesus
    who can bring us into an intimate relationship
        with God.
Our devotion to Mary must never diminish that.
61 But since she played such a pivotal role
    in the life and work of Jesus,
    we now realize that she is
    the first to receive the grace we also seek.
62 And even though Mary's place is subordinate to Jesus',
    nonetheless, we still understand her
    to be a great helper on our way to holiness.
63 By her belief and obedience
    and through the work of the Holy Spirit,
    she gave birth to Jesus and raised him with Joseph.
Her faith remained strong:
    Even though she must have faced temptations
    as Jesus himself did,
    she listened instead to God's promise.
64 Since Mary is the Mother of Jesus
    and we are sisters and brothers of Jesus,
    we can call Mary our mother as well.
How appropriate this is and how privileged we are
    to have such a mother:
        one who is eternally attentive to our struggles
        and always ready to nurture us spiritually!
The Church takes Mary as its example
    and always tries to imitate her life
        and always seeks to give birth
        to the presence of Jesus in the world.

Hence, the Church is also a mother to the faithful,
       bearing Christ for them,
              gently guiding them in life to a confident faith.
65 Therefore, the faithful now turn their eyes to Mary
       as the model of virtue.
By meditating on her, we grow more and more like her son
       and enter more intimately into the mystery
              of the Incarnation.
We honor Mary and have piety toward her
       so that we can know Jesus better
              and the whole world can be more open
              to receive the grace of Jesus Christ.
66 There is absolutely no other reason .
       for our devotion to Mary.
67 At no time should our devotion to Mary
       resemble the reverence and worship
       that we give to God.
We encourage Catholics to foster a loving devotion for Mary
       as our custom has been for so many centuries.
But at the same time,
       this council urges theologians and pastors
       to abstain both from gross exaggerations
       and neglectful omission
              in considering the dignity of Mary.
Our piety should be based on both Scripture
       and the long-standing Tradition of the Church
       and should follow Church teaching.
We should all be careful not to act in such a way
       that others will misunderstand us,
       especially other Christian Churches
              that might not foster
              such strong devotion to Mary.

68 Mary's place is with God in heaven.
69 This gives us great hope
       of what we ourselves can look forward to.
And so, with great longing and heartfelt trust,
       we bring our prayers to Mary
       and ask her to pray for us.
We know that she desires exactly what God desires
       and what we really want:
That in the end, all will be restored in Jesus the Christ,

and everyone will live in peace
with God and with one another.
Then we will honestly know what it means
to be the People of God.
Then we will fully understand
that Jesus, who is the Christ, is the Light of Nations.

The Dogmatic Constitution on Divine Revelation

From the Second Vatican Council
Promulgated by Pope Paul VI on November 18, 1965
Dei Verbum

Preface

1 This council now wishes to address the matter
      of how God reveals Godself to humankind
      and how humans respond to the voice of God.
This we do in order to strengthen the faith of all people.
It is our hope that by hearing the message of Jesus,
      all the world might believe,
      and, believing, might hope
      and, hoping, might love more profoundly.
In this, we take as our lead the words of St. John,
      expressed in the first letter,
      "What we have seen and heard,
         we announce to you
         so that you may have communion with us
         and together, our community
            may be with God
            and God's Son, Jesus Christ."

Chapter I:
Revelation itself

2 Out of total love for us humans,
      God chose to reveal himself
      and speak to us as friends.
God wants nothing less
      than that we come to know God fully:
      to know God's constant love,
      to understand God's unfathomable faithfulness,
      to experience God right down to the marrow.
This is what we mean when we speak of revelation:
      that we make plain and evident
      the realities of God who is
         so mysterious yet closer than our best friend.
In revealing God's inner self,

God does not merely reveal information
about the divine life,
but invites us into close companionship.
God actually shares with us the divine nature
so that we are no longer strangers to God
or to one another.
God shows us what God is really like,
and in this process, we come to know God's heart
as God knows ours.
This activity of God revealing Godself to us
occurs with both words and deeds
which have an inner unity:
The deeds of God in history
confirm the teaching signified by the words
while at the same time the words
proclaim the deeds
and interpret them for us!
Hence, the most profound truth about God shines out
for all to see;
indeed, our human connection with God
is made known in Christ!
Jesus the Christ is both the message and the messenger
of all that God wants to say to us.

3 From the beginning, God has been continually with us,
conscious of our human nature.
Hence, we pray, not to an absent and angry God,
living in a place far away from us,
but to a loving and caring God who is near to us.
How near? As near as our hearts and souls,
within and among us,
making himself known as the source of life.
God was first manifest in creation,
being known in wonder,
power,
majesty,
and goodness
through the created world.
Thus, all people have access to God
and all people can, on some level,
come to know of God's existence and inner self.
Over the course of history, though,

it has become more and more apparent to us
that God wishes to speak to us as friends,
>to live among us,
>and to invite us into a close union.
God called Abraham and Sarah and their offspring
>to enter into friendship with God
>and later called Moses and Miriam
>and on through the prophets . . .
>>. . . promising them divine closeness,
>>promising them salvation.

4 And then there was the Christ!
>Jesus who is the Christ was the full expression of God
>and he now dwells with us
>helping us understand the inner life of God.
Jesus proclaimed through his life and death,
>through his rising and remaining among us,
>that God is indeed with us,
>>to free us from the darkness of sin
>>and to raise us up to life eternal.
Everything that God wanted to say to us for all eternity
>was made known in Jesus, who is the Christ.
This was the perfect moment of divine revelation,
>and we await no further revelation of that kind
>except to know what the message of Jesus
>>demands of us:
>>and that is being revealed
>>>in every heart
>>>and in every age.

5 Nor are we left here all alone.
The Holy Spirit brings all this to completion in us
>by deepening our interior lives
>so that this revelation might take root there.
Thus, we are able to give free assent to these truths,
>our hearts moved and turned toward God,
>the eyes of our minds opened
>>by the Spirit.
6 Hence we can come to understand more fully
>those divine matters and persons
>which it is otherwise beyond us
>>to grasp!

Chapter II:
Handing on Divine Revelation

7 We believe that God has made it possible
        for the revealed truths about our lives
        to be fully and faithfully handed on forever.
Jesus, therefore, sent his followers
        to announce this Good News
        which they did in two ways:
        First, they preached and taught orally
           and observed a way of life
           based on Jesus' teaching.
        Second, they eventually wrote down the message,
           under the guidance of the Spirit.
Then they handed on the authority to teach
        to the first bishops who took their place.
The role of those early bishops
        was to keep the entire message of Christ
           together,
           complete,
           and intact
        for all generations to know and understand.
8 We believe it is God's plan that succeeding generations
        would have access to the Word of God
        through an unending succession
           of preaching and witnessing
           until the end of time.
The message passed along in this way
        contains everything needed to live a holy life.
This way of passing on the faith
        is like passing on an inheritance
        from one generation to the next.
           That which is most precious to the Church
           is lovingly guarded and, at the same time,
           generously and freely given
           to the daughters and sons of God.

Indeed this "deposit of faith," this Tradition,
        the Good News given by God,
        develops in the Church through the Holy Spirit.
Our faith is not a static reality, lifeless and dead.
Rather, over time, there is growth in understanding
        and development in doctrine.

This growth and development occur through contemplation,
    as well as through study
    and putting belief into action,
    producing penetrating and fresh insights into faith.
Even the Scriptures themselves
    are more fully understood over time,
    each age hearing it as a living voice
        for that particular time.

9 Hence, there is a very close connection
    between Scripture, on the one hand,
    and Church tradition, on the other.
They both flow from the same divine well
    and share the same goal.
Scripture is that written message which is the Word of God,
    of which we have two volumes:
    the Old Testament and the New Testament.
Sacred tradition is how that message
    is passed on to us through
        liturgy,
        prayers,
        the teachings of the apostles,
        and the truths not fully explained in Scripture.
We, therefore, honor both sources of knowledge:
    Sacred Scripture and sacred tradition.
"Consequently, it is not from Sacred Scripture alone
    that the Church draws her certainty
    about everything which has been revealed."

10 In sum, we believe that Sacred Scripture and tradition
    form one sacred deposit or message from God to us.
Today it is the task of the Church
    to keep the Word of God alive.
    In all we say and all we do in our everyday lives,
    this Word of God grows more vibrant in the world.
Everyone who is baptized is empowered
    to understand the Word of God
    and to find meaning for their lives in this Word.
Bishops have a particularly important role
    in bringing the Word of God to light.
It is their role, in fact, to provide for authentic and uniform
    interpretation of the Word of God.

Thus, neither the Church as a whole
      nor any teacher of the Church
      is above the Word of God.
These three, then, are intimately linked:
      Sacred Scripture,
      tradition,
      and the teaching of the Church.

Chapter III:
Sacred Scripture:
Its Divine Inspiration and Interpretation

11 Those who wrote down the words of Scripture
      were inspired by the Holy Spirit.
The Holy Spirit guided the writers
      so that they recorded God's revelation to us.
At the same time, these writers
      had full use of their intelligence,
         their hearts,
         their insights,
         and their everyday experiences.
They were not mindless scribes,
      unaware of what they were writing.
It is as though they were so in tune with the Holy Spirit
      that everything that they chose to write
      was exactly what needed to be written.
Therefore, we believe that the books of Scripture
      teach solidly, faithfully, and without error
         everything that God wants them to teach.

12 However, those who read these words today
      must study them carefully
      in order to understand the original message of God.
It is, therefore, necessary for today's readers
      to investigate what the writers intended to say.
There are, for example, various forms of literature
      used in the Scriptures:
         historical,
         prophetic,
         poetic,
         and others.
In addition, there were circumstances
      in the days of the writers

which differ from today's world and culture.
In order to understand the words of Scripture,
  one must understand these factors
  and how they influenced the text.
Not only that, but we must also be careful to consider
  Scripture as a whole
  and not in fractions and broken parts.
13 The words of Scripture, after all, are human words
  imbued with the truth and holiness of God,
    and we must scrutinize them carefully
    to understand them fully.

Chapter IV:
The Old Testament

14 God chose the people of Israel to form a sacred nation
  united by the covenant of love.
God revealed Godself so that the people of Israel
  could experience divine love
  and be a beacon of light to other nations.
As we have already said,
  God's revelation began among the Hebrew people
  when Abraham and Sarah were called forth.
God's word was also made known through others,
  especially Moses and the prophets.
The books of the Old Testament preserve this memory
  of God's loving goodness to a people in slavery.
These books of the Old Testament
  remain permanently valuable
  because they tell the story of God's great love for us.
15 They contain a store of marvelous teachings about God,
  wholesome wisdom about human life,
  and a beautiful treasury of prayers.
In all of this, the mystery of our salvation is present
  in a hidden way.
    Christians should receive these books with reverence.
16 The two testaments are intimately linked,
  the New hidden in the Old,
  and the Old made manifest in the New.

Chapter V:
The New Testament

17 Jesus revealed the Reign of God among us

and helped us see and know God intimately.
Jesus showed us who God really is
  and completed his work by his self-giving love,
  which showed us the way of God.
Death has no power over love, we learned from Jesus,
  and this divine power is also given to us
  as sons and daughters of God.
The writings of the New Testament stand as God's witness
  to this marvelous reality.

18 Among the many books of Scripture,
  the Gospels have special prominence.
They are our primary way of knowing
  about the words and deeds of Jesus, the Christ.
The message they contain, in fact,
  is the foundation of our Faith.
There is really only one Gospel—
  the Gospel of Jesus, the Christ.
  But this one gospel is given voice
  in four distinct books:
    Matthew, Mark, Luke, and John.

19 The Gospels are a written account
  of the stories and memories of Jesus.
They are not meant as historical records;
  they aren't a biography of Jesus as such.
Instead, the authors chose some stories
  from among the many which they had in hand
    reducing some to a summary
    and synthesizing others.
They wrote to a particular audience in a particular location
  addressing the needs of that community
  and highlighting elements of Jesus' teaching
    which applied there most specifically.
They drew their material from their own memories,
  from the witness of others who knew Jesus,
  and from stories told about him in the early Church.
Taken as a whole, the Gospels reveal the teaching of Jesus
  and help us see how close God is to us.
20 The letters of St. Paul
  and other apostolic writings
  are also contained in the New Testament

and all of them serve to more and more fully
reveal the work of Christ.

Chapter VI:
Sacred Scripture in the Life of the Church

21 The Church venerates
      sacred Scripture and the Body of Jesus the Christ
      with the same vigor.
Both of these are celebrated in our Liturgy.
The bread of life we are offered at Mass
      flows both from God's Word and from Jesus' Body.
The altar around which we gather at Mass
      is really both the table of the Word of God
      and the table of the Body of Jesus, the Christ.
All the teaching of the Church
      is nourished and focused, therefore,
            by sacred Scripture.
In Scripture, God meets us and speaks to us
      with great love.
The force and power of the Word of God
      is so great that it stands
      as the support and energy of the whole Church,
            the strength of faith for its members,
            food for the soul,
            and the pure source of spiritual life.

22 Because this is true,
      easy access to Scripture
      should be provided to all the faithful.
Toward this end, new translations should be prepared
      in all the languages of the world.
We encourage cooperation
      among the various Christian Churches
      in preparing accurate translations of Scripture.

23 This council urges the study of Sacred Scripture,
      of the Fathers of both East and West,
      and of the language and message of the liturgy.
Biblical scholars, working under the care of the Church,
      should make the texts accessible
      to as many as possible.
24 The authentic study of theology rests, after all,

on Scripture together with sacred tradition.
Theology is made more robust and understandable
when we scrutinize the truth of Jesus, the Christ
        for surely, Jesus is the source of our faith.
Likewise, Scripture takes its place in all of catechesis,
    in preaching, teaching, and instruction.

25 Indeed, all who work in the Church
        must be fully trained in the Scriptures
        and must use them as the basis of preaching,
            catechesis,
            and Christian instruction.
The faithful as well should know Scripture,
        for through the words of these texts, they meet Jesus.
Bishops should take on the work
        of making Scripture available
        and of making it understandable to their flocks.
Even non-Christians should have access to sacred Scripture.

26 Just as the life of the Church is strengthened
        through more frequent celebration of the Eucharist,
        so it will be stimulated
        by a growing reverence for the Word of God.

The Pastoral Constitution on the Church in the Modern World

From the Second Vatican Council
Promulgated by Pope Paul VI on December 8, 1965

Gaudium et Spes

Preface

1 "The joys and hopes, the griefs and anxieties
    of the [people] of this age,
    especially those who are poor
    or in any way afflicted:
        these are the joys and hopes,
           the griefs and anxieties,
           of the followers of Christ.
Indeed, nothing genuinely human
    fails to raise an echo in their hearts."
The Christian community
    is, after all, a community of women and men
    genuinely linked with humankind and its history,
        bearing a message of salvation
        intended for all people.
2 This council, therefore,
    having already looked in depth at the Church itself,
    now turns its attention on the whole of humanity.
We want to state clearly our understanding
    of the presence and function of the Church
    in the world of today.
For the world is the theater of human history,
    its energies, tragedies, and triumphs.
The Christian vision is that the world was created
    and is sustained by God.
It was learned the way of God's love from Jesus.
It is now being re-created and brought to its destiny
    under the Holy Spirit.
3 We now offer to the world
    the honest assistance of the Church
    in fostering human harmony which is our destiny.
In this, we follow our teacher, Jesus the Christ,

who came to give witness to the truth
and to serve and not be served.
People today are troubled and perplexed
by questions about their lives in the world,
about their place in the universe,
about the meaning of individual and collective work,
and about the purpose and nature
of being human.
We now wish to enter into dialogue
with the whole human family about all this.
We will clarify these questions
in the light of the gospel
and offer the human race the saving resources
of the Church.
Our entire subject is humankind,
men and women:
whole and entire
with body and soul,
with heart and conscience,
with mind and will.

Therefore, we in this Council offer everyone the assurance
that we are in solidarity with you.
We have no temporal ambition
except to foster love and peace,
and to serve all men and women of the world.

Introductory Statement
about the situation of people in the world

4 In order to proceed here,
we must understand the world in which we live—
its expectations and longings
and its often-dramatic ways.
We must, in other words, scrutinize the signs of the times
and interpret them in the light of the Gospel.
In language understandable for each generation,
the Church should be able to give
meaningful answers to questions
that people have about life:
both now and after death.
One of those signs
is the profound and rapid change

which is everywhere.
Riding on the intelligence of the human race,
    the creative energies of people
      have produced unprecedented social transformation.
As we might expect, this transformation
    has also brought serious difficulties.
Never has the human race enjoyed more wealth,
    yet a huge number of people are tormented
      by poverty, illiteracy, and want.
Never has there been such human freedom in the world,
    yet new forms of social and psychological slavery
      also make their appearance alongside it.
Never has the world been so close
    to the brink of unity and interdependence,
    yet new and opposing camps
      threaten this possibility.
There is even the frightening prospect
    of a war of total destruction!
Never before has the drive for a better world
    been more on the minds of men and women
    yet there is not a corresponding
      spiritual advancement
      to give it meaning and guidance.
As a result, many people are burdened with uneasiness
    even as they enjoy the benefits of modern life.
We humans must respond to all of this;
    indeed, we cannot escape doing so.

5 Today's spiritual hunger results, in part,
    from a much more scientific approach
    to understanding the culture and society.
Technology is transforming the world,
    not to mention outer space!
And to a certain extent, the human intellect
    is even beginning to control time:
      the past by means of historical knowledge,
      the future by means
        of projecting and planning.
Likewise, advances in the social sciences,
    including biology, psychology, and others,
    bring us hope of improved self-knowledge.
At the same time,

the human race is now considering the regulation
of its own population growth.
History speeds along on so rapid a course
that one can scarcely keep abreast of it,
and we humans have now passed
from a rather static understanding of reality
to one much more dynamic
and evolutionary!
6 By this very fact, local groups,
such as families, clans, or villages,
are rapidly being transformed.
Ideas and social conditions which have lasted for centuries
are quickly being replaced in our time
by new concepts of social organization.
City living is much more common today, for example,
and even rural places have city-like lifestyles.
New and incredibly efficient media
make connections around the world possible
so that styles of thought and feeling
that were once limited in their scope
can be known worldwide.
Migration is increasing as well,
and this creates a socialization
which doesn't always include personal relationships.
And while what we describe here is true
in advanced nations,
it is rapidly becoming truer worldwide.

7 So much change calls traditional values into question,
especially among young people
who are not satisfied to wait until adulthood
to take their role in this dynamic.
Hence, the handing down of teachings and traditions
is more difficult than ever before.
Religion is also affected, of course,
by this new world movement.
On one hand, superstitious and magical views of the world
are eradicated by science and knowledge
which purifies faith in the unseen God.
On the other hand, growing numbers of people
are abandoning religion
in favor of science or humanism.

Evidence of this disturbing trend is found in many places:
    in literature, art, humanities, history, and law.

8 All these modern developments,
        coming so rapidly and disorderly,
        intensify imbalances within the human person.
One's intellect, for example, may be thoroughly modern,
        while one's theory of meaning is more traditional,
            and no joining of the two seems possible.
Or one's concern for practicality and efficiency
        is in tension with one's moral conscience.
Or the demands of collective existence
        conflict with one's need for personal thought,
            or even contemplation.
Furthermore, the family is in tension
        with pressures on it from many sides:
            population control,
            economic realities,
            or social demands.
Likewise, tensions emerge between nations
        when some are so wealthy and others so poor.
All of this leads to mistrust, division, and hardship,
        and humans are at once the cause and the victims.

9 For the first time in history,
        many believe it is possible and desirable
        that the benefits of modern culture
            can be extended to everyone.
And those who do not have these benefits yet want them,
        especially the world's starving people,
        but also women, workers, and farmers.
There is also a movement for a universal community
        in which persons can live a full and free life.
In all of this, the modern world is both powerful and weak,
        capable of noble deeds or foul ones,
        in the path of freedom or that of slavery.
Modern people seek new levels of meaning today
        precisely because of the unleashed powers
        of modern life
        which can either serve us or destroy us.

10 The modern condition is rooted

in the nature of human life itself:
boundless in ambition yet limited,
attracted to many things,
but forced to choose among them,
often choosing those things
known to be harmful.
Many who choose practical materialism
do not even give this matter any thought!
Others are weighed down by unhappiness
and do not have the emotional wherewithal
to consider it.
Still others believe human effort alone
is sufficient to order society
and bring meaning and peace to humankind.
And some believe there is no meaning in life to begin with.
Yet there are those, increasing in number, who ask
"What is a human person?
What is this sense of sorrow,
of evil and death,
which continues to exist despite progress?
What victory have we won in these times
and at what cost?
What can we expect from life?
what can we offer to it?
What follows our earthly life?"

We in the Church firmly believe
that the light of Jesus can illumine our search.
Beneath these many changes and developments
is an unchanging and loving God
and we now speak of these matters
in order to cooperate in finding the solution
to the outstanding problems of our age.

Part 1:
The Church and Humankind's Vocation

11 We begin our inquiry with the People of God
which believes it is led by the Holy Spirit.
This People of God,
this human family of which we are part,
makes a careful inquiry into the events,
needs,

and desires of this age
　　　to find authentic signs of God's presence here:
Who are we humans, anyway?
　　　　What does society need today to be better?
　　　　What do human actions throughout the world mean?
People are waiting for answers to these questions,
　　　and by this inquiry, it will become clear
　　　that the Church and the world
　　　　　render service to each other.
This is so because the mission of the Church is religious,
　　　but it is also supremely human!

Chapter I:
The Dignity of the Human Person

12 Pretty much everyone in every part of the planet believes
　　　with unanimous opinion
　　　that the human person is the center and crown of life.
But what is the human person?
There are divergent views among people about this,
　　　some exalting the human person
　　　as the measure of all things
　　　　and others debasing human nature
　　　　to the point of despair.
We take a positive view of the human person,
　　　based on the words of our Scriptures
　　　expressed in the Book of Genesis
　　　that God created us in the divine likeness
　　　　and was pleased with the outcome.
We understand ourselves, furthermore,
　　　to be primarily social creatures,
　　　created from the beginning to have companions.

13 But there is more.
The human person was slow to learn how to hear
　　　the voice of God echoing within
　　　and obey his or her conscience.
This caused us to separate from each other,
　　　to doubt each other's love and faithfulness.
It caused us to be dishonest when confronted,
　　　and to believe we could live somehow
　　　without the guiding voice we hear
　　　　in that place where we are alone with God

whose voice nevertheless echoes within us.
Human experience agrees with this:
for when we examine our hearts,
we do indeed find an inclination toward
disrupted relationships and darkness.
We find ourselves split within ourselves,
caught in a dramatic struggle of good versus evil,
light versus darkness.
And into this situation,
Jesus appeared as the Christ,
the anointed one of God,
the Light of the World,
to strengthen us with grace
to free us from this darkness
and to help us hear God's voice again.

14 For the human person,
although composed of both body and soul,
is a unified, whole person, not divided.
We are obliged to love our bodies and, indeed,
the whole material world
for it is created by God, too.
Nevertheless, it is often there,
in the material, physical realm,
that we find inclinations toward darkness.
So, we must probe our human nature to its depth
to find our souls for there in the depth of our hearts,
we also find God.

15 We can conclude from this plunging into our depths
that in some ways
we humans surpass the material universe
and share in the light of the divine mind.
We have made great progress in many areas,
using our talents,
and we continue to win enormous victories
in science, technology, and the liberal arts.
Nonetheless, we continue to search
for penetrating truths—and to find them!
We can look beyond observable data
and employ the wisdom
which perfects our intelligence,

and it is this wisdom which we now need so badly
or the world may perish.
Wise men and women must come forth to lead us in this age,
and they may well come from less developed places
where wisdom often thrives.
This wisdom leads us to desire goodness and truth.

16 In the depths of our conscience,
we detect a law and a truth
which we have not laid upon ourselves
but which we must obey.
Its voice, ever calling us to love
and to do what is good and avoid evil,
sounds in our heart at the right moment.
For we have in our hearts a law or a truth
which has been carved into us by God.
Our very dignity comes from observing this inner law,
and by it, we will be judged.
Our conscience is our most secret core and sanctuary.
There we are alone with God
whose voice echoes in our depths.
The voice we hear will always, in a variety of ways,
call us to love God and neighbor well.
By being faithful to it,
we are joined with all of humanity
in a great human search for truth
and for genuine solutions
to the vexing problems of modern life.
It is clear from what we are saying here
that we must be faithful, then, to that inner voice,
that "divine guide" in our souls,
and not allow our clarity to be dulled
by repeated acts that are contrary to love.
We must not allow our souls
to be nibbled away by acts of hate and selfishness.

17 The key to this is freedom.
Authentic human freedom does not mean
"doing whatever we please."
Instead, it flows from attentive listening to God
as he speaks within our consciences,
but also in doing what our conscience directs.

Such free choices will always be fully human ones
     and will not result from impulsive actions
          or from external rules.
We humans have the potential
     to spontaneously choose Good
     with God as our inner guide.

18 It is in the face of death
     that all this is brought into sharp relief and focus
     for death eventually claims us all
          and none of our technology can stop it.
And even if we could prolong life,
     we would still be possessed of an innate sense
     of a higher life in divine love.
For we believe that God created us for eternal life
     where the wholeness we lose through sin
          will be restored because of the mercy of Christ.
Faith, therefore, fills thoughtful people with hope
     and unites them with all who have already died.

19 For our lives flow from the creative energy of this faith
     and return there as well
          in an intimate and eternal linkage.
Because we believe this link with God
     is vital for human happiness and fulfillment,
     we want to examine atheism in all its forms.
We consider it one of the most serious problems of this age.
There are many kinds of atheism —
     some very subtle forms and others more blatant.
There are those, for example,
     who expressly deny the existence of God
     while others simply argue
     that we can know nothing at all about God.
Others believe that all truths can be explained by reason
     or even that there is no absolute truth to explain
          in the first place!
Some hold humanity in such high regard
     that they have left only an anemic faith in God
     though they may not deny God outrightly.
And still others simply have no religious stirrings,
     no desire to ask these questions at all.

20 Modern atheism confuses human freedom
> with our relationship to God
> as though the two cannot coexist.
It claims that men and women will be freed
> only by economic gains or social advancement.

21 But we believe and have always taught
> that the true nature of humans
> is to be joined with the divine life force,
>> and that real freedom comes in this.
We continue to teach this,
> and we assert firmly that any other approach
> robs human persons of their dignity
> and offers them only economic or social solutions
>> to situations demanding more!
But, while we believe strongly in what we teach here,
> we also reject the distinction we sometimes see
> between believers and unbelievers.
This distinction often results in the stripping away
> of the human rights of the unbelievers.
We call for religious liberty in this regard
> and hope we can all work together
>> to build a better world.
With true courtesy, we invite atheists to examine the Gospel
> with an open mind.
22 We believe that believing in divine love
> does not diminish human life here and now
> but propels us to live with high nobility
>> because when we die, we take with us
>> that love—that divine love—
>> that we have in our hearts.
Without this hope, indeed, the riddles of life and death,
> of guilt and of grief, go unresolved
>> and people often succumb to despair.
Our lives remain unsolved puzzles,
> especially when major life events unfold for us
> and we come to understand ourselves
>> more and more only with the wisdom of God.
So, the remedy which we apply to atheism is twofold:
> the proper presentation of the Church's teaching
> and well-lived Christian lives.
People will see us believers,

as they did the martyrs and others in the past;
they will see our unity and charity,
and come to believe themselves.

For us Christians, the truth and meaning of our lives
is wrapped up in the mystery of Jesus the Christ,
the Incarnate Word of God.
In Jesus, anointed as the Christ,
the riddles of sorrow and death take on meaning,
the divine presence is made profoundly clear,
and we find the energy and power to live fully.
In Jesus, we become capable of being fully human,
sharing in the full divinity which is made flesh,
working with human hands,
thinking with a human mind,
acting by human choice,
and, above all, loving with a human heart.
What greater love do we need?
What greater truth?
The mystery of the human person
is centered in this divine core,
revealed through Jesus, the Christ,
and stirring us to full humanity.
Such is the mystery of being human—and it is a great one!
The riddles of life and death become clear, however,
when we allow ourselves to believe
that light shines on in the darkness,
and that love cannot be ended with death.

Chapter II:
The Community of Humankind

23 There is a growing interdependence among people today
which is based on the many technological advances
which are apparent to everyone.
But this interdependence reaches its perfection
only in growing *human* relationships,
not merely scientific ones.
For God, we believe, desires that all people
become one family
with love for God and neighbor as the basis.
We cannot separate these two:
whoever loves God must love neighbor

or the claim to love is false.
Jesus said as much himself.
It is obvious how important this is
 as we come to rely more on each other
  and grow in unity.
Because of Jesus' prayer
 "that all may be one as we are one,"
 new horizons are now opened for us
 implying that we will reach our true destiny
 only by pursuing such oneness with each other.
25 So we humans, in order to fully discover ourselves,
 must donate ourselves to one another in love.
This aspect of human nature, the social aspect,
 suggests strongly that the advance of society
 depends on individual persons progressing first.
After all, the whole purpose of social organizations
 is to make human life nobler.
This social nature of which we speak
 makes it clear that the progress of the human person
 and the advance of society go hand in hand.
After all, the whole purpose of social institutions
 such as the family,
  political parties,
  labor organizations,
  and even the churches
 is to enhance our lives as human persons.
Indeed, some of these social institutions
 arise from the very intrinsic nature of being human.
  The family is one of these
  as is the political community.
Other social institutions are created by us
 to serve our needs,
 and our participation in them is more voluntary.
And both of these are on the rise today,
 increasing both in number and influence.
Even though this is true, however, it is also true today
 that men and women are often diverted
 from doing good and spurred toward doing evil
  and the cause of this is the very social order
   in which they live
   and into which they have been born.
There are natural tensions in any social plan,

especially economic life,
>political organization,
>and various social groups.
It is these tensions which often yield to a breakdown
>in human nature
>based on human pride and selfishness
>>which contaminate these social activities.
>>Selfishness results.
Sin can be overcome only by adopting self-giving love
>and that can only happen with the help of grace.
26 There is a condition in human life which we call
>"the common good."
By this term, we refer
>to that set of conditions in human life—
>economic, social, political, and others—
>which, taken together, makes it possible for us
>>to become all we are created to be,
>>and to reach our human fulfillment.
Various social groups
>approach the common good differently
>and must take each other into account, therefore,
>>if all humanity is to achieve it.
We recognize with increasing awareness today
>that there is a fundamental human dignity
>which must be in place for the common good
>to be possible in the first place.
This fundamental human dignity
>is universal and unchanging,
>based as it is in our created nature.
It leads us to say that everyone must have
>food, clothing, and shelter;
>the right to choose a state of life freely;
>the right to found a family;
>the right to education, employment,
>>a good reputation, respect,
>>and appropriate information;
>the right to follow one's own conscience,
>to the protection of privacy
>and to rightful freedom,
>>even in matters of religion.
Our point is becoming clearer here:
>all social organizing must be for the benefit

of the human person,
and it requires constant improvement.
It must be founded on truth and built on justice;
it must be animated by love and freedom.
And we realize that, in order for this to be true today,
substantial adjustments in attitude
and abundant changes in current society
will have to take place.
But we believe that God's Spirit
hovers with us and helps us
to renew the face of the earth.
And, furthermore, we believe that it is rooted
in the very heart of men and women
to seek increasing dignity,
and not to sink into darkness.

27 In practical terms, this means
that everyone must consider his or her neighbor,
without exception, "another self."
Each person must take into account first of all
the life of each other person
and the means necessary to live with dignity.
It must not be with us as it was with the nameless rich man
who saw Lazarus bleeding and hungry,
without this dignity of which we speak here,
and ignored him.
Remember what happened?
Lazarus rested in the bosom of Abraham and Sarah
while that rich man created his own hell
and lived in selfishness and ignorance for eternity.
In our times, this means we have a special obligation
to make ourselves the neighbor of every person
without exception
and to actively assist them when we meet them
in the paths of our lives.
This includes old people abandoned by all,
foreigners in our midst,
refugees,
children without parents,
and those who hunger and thirst.
All of these, when we see them and hear their cry,
disturb our conscience

and remind us of Jesus' teaching in Matthew 25:
> "As long as you did it for one of these,
> ... you did it for me."

And not only that.
We must also work to defeat any force opposed to life itself,
>   such as any kind of murder,
>>   genocide,
>>   abortion,
>>   euthanasia,
>>   or willful self-destruction.

We must work to defeat
>   whatever violates human dignity,
>   such as mutilation,
>>   mental or physical torture,
>>   coercion of the will,
>>   subhuman living conditions,
>>   arbitrary imprisonment,
>>   deportation,
>>   slavery,
>>   prostitution,
>>   the selling of women and children,
>>   and disgraceful working conditions.

All of these poison human society,
>   doing harm to both those afflicted by them
>   and those perpetrating them.

They are, in short, a supreme dishonor to the Creator God.

28 We should also have respect and love
>   for those who think differently than we do
>   in social,
>>   political,
>>   or even religious matters.

In fact, the more deeply we understand others,
>   the more we can dialogue with them,
>   seeking understanding.

This is not to say we should accept untruth as truth
>   or meanness as goodness.

But the people whom we believe to be in untruth
>   are dignified nonetheless,
>   and we teach that only God can make judgments
>>   in the end.

God alone is the searcher of the human heart,

and we should not make judgments
    about the internal guilt of anyone.
To the contrary, we are taught by Jesus to love
    even those we consider our enemies.

29 Every person has a soul and is created in God's image.
    All people are of the same nature and origin.
Having been offered a unique relationship
    As son and daughters of God,
    all of us likewise have the same divine calling.
There is a fundamental equality of all human persons
    regardless of social or cultural background,
        race,
        gender,
        color,
        language,
        or religion.
All discrimination should be overcome and eradicated,
    and we regret that so many human rights
    are not being honored around the world,
        especially for women who are not free
            to choose a husband freely,
            to embrace a state of life,
            to acquire an education,
            or to enjoy cultural benefits
                equal to men.
As we have made clear above,
    human institutions, both private and public,
    must labor to enhance the dignity and purpose
        of all women and men.

30 A purely private sense of morality
    cannot exist in this day and age
    because of the interdependence we have
        on one another.
Each of us must not only fulfill our human call
    to live justly and with love
    but must also work to ensure
        that social institutions are fairer.
Each of us contributes to the common good
    when we use our abilities in this way.
We should pay our just share of taxes,

obey social laws,
and conduct our business honestly.
We should operate our industry with an eye to
the protection of human health around us.
It even comes down to obeying speed limits
so that those around us are not in danger.
31 In sum, we call on everyone to consider it
his or her sacred obligation
to esteem and observe social needs.
If all do, a genuinely new and more humane society
will be available to all.
For this to happen, education must be widespread,
especially for youth of every background.
Likewise, neither destitution nor sumptuousness is our aim
but the building up of the common good.
Hence, the desire to take part in organizing society
should be encouraged for everyone,
and we offer special praise for those nations
which allow the fullest possible participation
in governance and public affairs.
32 Once again we point out that God did not create humans
to live in isolation but in community.
We are not individuals set side by side
without bonds or links,
but rather, we are bound together as a single people,
with one common inner principle—the Spirit.
This communal nature of ours
finds its fullest expression in Jesus
who lived in radical human fellowship.
The lifestyle, friendships, and social engagements of Jesus
point the way for us:
we are to live as one Body,
members of one another,
rendering mutual service
to each other based on our gifts.
And this communal solidarity in Jesus
must be increased steadily
until we live fully with God as one family.

Chapter III:
Human Activity throughout the World
33 Men and women have ceaselessly worked

to improve their lives
using their talents and hard work to do so.
Today that work is paying off more than ever,
and nearly every aspect of human life
has come under our control
through science and technology.
Little by little the worldwide human family
is realizing that it is indeed a family
united by common concerns.
The result of this is that many phenomena
which were once attributed to divine power
are now fully understood to be of human making.
But all of this leaves us with certain nagging questions
about life, meaning, and the end goal of it all.

The Church stands in the midst of these questions
and offers guidance without having all the solutions.
The Church can offer principles for proceeding
and wants to add to the human journey
the light of truth
so that we do not wander in darkness.

34 Christians are convinced that the triumphs
of human endeavor,
the wonderful advances of society,
and the monumental efforts to produce a better world
are completely in accord with God's will.
It is the very mission of the human person
to understand and use the benefits of creation
to the good of all.
Therefore, in everyday life,
as well as in more dramatic ways,
when we work for our livelihoods,
God is present, unfolding ongoing creative work.
Hence, far from thinking that such human advances
are in opposition to God's desires,
we are convinced they are a sign of God's grace.
We, therefore, say with confidence
that we are not hindered from improving the world
by the Christian message
but, on the contrary, bound to do just that.

35 Human activity, to be sure,
      flows from people and benefits people.
When someone works, he or she alters things and society,
      but he or she also develops her or his very self.
In a word, a worker grows,
      and this growth is more valuable
      than the external wealth it produces.
A person is more precious for what she or he is
      than for what he or she has.
Likewise, then, we also believe
      that whatever is done to obtain justice,
         to establish broader solidarity,
         and to make living conditions more humane
            is more valuable than technology.
We can, therefore, draw this principle from our thinking:
      all human endeavor is of God
      when it allows men and women
         to pursue their created purpose
         and follow it to fulfillment.

36 Many modern people seem to fear
      that a closer bond
      between human activity and religion
         will work against independence in science.
We have sometimes even been led by certain Christians
      to believe that faith and science oppose one another
      but we do not agree with this at all.
The profound realities of society and science
      are deciphered by us little by little,
      and this gradual discovery of the universe
         is our natural instinct
         and also, we believe, God's will.
Whoever works to learn about the world in this way,
      even if they are unaware of it,
      is nevertheless being led by the hand of God
         in whom everything continues in being
         and finds its ultimate meaning.
If such methodological study is carried out
      in a genuinely scientific way
      following moral norms, then it is of God.
But if the scientist denies the place of the divine
      in his or her work, it is false

because apart from the Creator,
creation no longer exists.
When God is forgotten, human life loses meaning.

37 We know from our Scriptures and our history
that we humans seem bound to wrestle constantly
with selfish desires.
When these self-centered ways of behaving emerge in us,
they threaten the peace and security of our race,
and this is especially true today.
Hence the world has not yet become a place
of true sister and brotherhood.
So we must wrestle with dark desires
made manifest in a spirit of vanity and malice,
and it is at this very point that the Church
offers us a helping hand.
In order to overcome this tendency toward darkness,
we must come to Jesus, the Christ.
By this we mean, our motives and actions
are made purer and more perfect
when we realize that everything we have
comes from God
and is intended for us to share.
Such an attitude makes us free and humble:
free to receive everything
and humble to know its source is not ourselves.

38 Jesus has shown us the way of love,
and the law of love is the fundamental law
of human growth, development, and transformation.
To those who believe in divine love,
Jesus has shown that the hope of a world
based on love is not a foolish hope.
This hope must be pursued in ordinary, everyday life
as we "lay down our lives" for one another,
having learned to do this from Jesus
and believing that doing so
will lead all to a glorious shared life.
Jesus is present in the midst of this,
providing the energy we need,
arousing the desire for good in us,
animating our hearts,

and purifying our noble longings
        for human solidarity.
This work is done by Jesus in the hearts of people
        by the power of the Holy Spirit.
This Spirit first arouses in us
        the desire for a better world
        but also encourages the best and most noble
                of our sentiments
                so they will be used toward this end:
                        to make love present.
And this divine, loving presence of Jesus
        is nowhere more profound
        than in the Eucharist itself
                where indeed the natural elements
                of bread and wine
                are changed into a meal of solidarity!

39 All of this is so important to us because of our belief
        that the world in which we now live
                is but a foreshadowing of what is to come.
We believe that the betterment of this world
        is God's will and desire
        for it makes us humans nobler
                and prepares us for an eternity
                on this same path of wholeness and holiness.

Chapter IV:
The Role of the Church in the Modern World
40 Everything we have said about the human person—
        about human dignity,
        human community,
        and the meaning of human activity—
                now serves as the foundation
                for what we wish to say here.
We will speak about the place of the Church in the world
        and the dialogue between them.
As we make our comments now,
        we also base them on what we have said
        about the nature of the Church
                as a sign to the world of the presence of God.
The Church, as we have already said,
        emerges from God's love for us

and God's desire that we form a divine family
during our lifetimes.
The Church is thus a leaven and a soul for human society
and, as such, that part of the Church
which is found among us now
and that part which is to come later
penetrate each other.
This is most evident in the Church's task
of elevating and healing the dignity of being human
and insisting on this point,
even in the face of darkness.
The Church offers deep meaning and purpose
to those who hear her word
and contributes to making the human family
more human!
This is a two-way relationship:
the Church assists the world,
and the world assists the Church.
And this applies to the Roman Catholic Church
but also to other Church bodies
who have the same goal.
41 We now intend to set forth certain principles
for the proper fostering of this mutual exchange
between the churches and the world.

Members of the human family today
are on the road to a more thorough development
of their personalities
and to a growing discovery and absolute claim
on fundamental human rights.
These are the ultimate goals of being human
and are written on the heart;
they are part and parcel of life,
the fundamental meaning of existence,
and the innermost nature of humankind.
We believe that only God can lead us to this truth;
only God provides an answer to the riddle of life.
The Church is a stable force
which steadfastly maintains human dignity
even in the face of fluctuating trends in society
regarding the value of life and the human body.
No one can protect humans from exploitation

better than those who speak for God,
and today that is the gospel of Christ,
entrusted to the Church.
The gospel has a sacred reverence
for the dignity of conscience
and its freedom of choice.
It announces and proclaims the freedom
of the sons and daughters of God,
and it rejects wholeheartedly all forms of slavery,
internal and external,
which result from human mistakes.
By virtue of this gospel,
the Church proclaims the rights of humankind.
It acknowledges and affirms those movements today
which support and foster these rights,
desiring to penetrate them
with the spirit of the gospel
so that we do not wander into the belief
that our rights are ensured
only when we are also free of divine law.
Indeed, divine law is most natural to humans
and without it the dignity of the human person
will perish.

42 The Church is not tied to any specific system
of government, economics, or social order.
The purpose which Jesus gave the Church
is, indeed, only a religious one.
Our mission is to provide light
to help guide others on their way.
As a matter of fact, the Church can and should
undertake certain works herself,
such as assisting the poor and suffering.
We see an evolution toward unity in the world today
which pleases us
because the innermost nature
of the Church is the promotion of unity.
And, since the Church is committed
to no single system of governance,
she can bridge them all, serving as a catalyst.
We, therefore, urge all women and men
to put strife and division aside

and live together in peace.
This council looks with great respect on all that is true,
    good, and just in social systems everywhere.
The Church is willing to promote and assist these systems
    and has no fiercer desire than to develop freely
    under every system which grants recognition
        to the fundamental rights of person and family
        and the demands of the common good.

43 We Christians believe that these times and this life
    will ultimately end in an eternal dwelling place.
Nonetheless, we also believe that life in this world
    and in these times must be lived nobly, fully,
    and with attention to our day-to-day obligations.
And we also believe that religion and everyday life
    are intimately and indissolubly linked,
    part and parcel of each other.
        We cannot divorce what happens in religion
        from how we live our everyday life.
Simply put, there is no split between faith
    and everyday life.
Jesus himself repeatedly warned against
    dividing life and religious belief in this way.
So did the prophets of the time before Jesus!
Therefore, let there be no false distinctions
    between one's professional and social life
    and one's religious life.
If you neglect your temporal duties,
    you also neglect your spiritual ones!
It behooves us Christians, then,
    to become skilled at our trades,
    to pay attention to developing expertise,
        and to use it wisely.
Lay people ought to follow their well-formed consciences
    so that the divine law is lived out in everyday life,
        looking to priests for spiritual nourishment,
        but not imagining they have all the answers!
And when faithful people disagree,
    and that will undoubtedly be the case,
    do not presume to speak for God or the Church
        but try to enlighten one another
        through honest discussion and charity,

always earnest in your search for truth.
In this way, laypeople, guided by their pastors
    who are guided by their bishops,
    will indeed animate the world with a Christian spirit.
Pastors and bishops, therefore,
    must remember that their daily conduct
    reflects the gospel and greatly influences others.
We believe the Church has always been
    a faithful lover of Jesus
    and an everlasting sign of salvation.
But we are also aware that some of her pastors,
    as well as laypeople,
    have not always been faithful to this love;
        some have failed to live out the very message
        which they are bound to preach!
However history judges them,
    we should be aware of this
    and work to improve such failings,
        purifying and renewing ourselves
        so that the light of Christ
        can indeed shine through us all!

44 As we have just described it,
    the Church can add significantly
    to the modern world,
    but the modern world
        can also benefit the Church.
The progress of science
    and the treasures hidden in various forms
        of human culture
        reveal new roads to truth.
The Church wants to speak in the language of the people
    and needs the help of those
    versed in varying specialties
        to do this.
Because change occurs so rapidly today
    and thought patterns differ so widely,
    the Church needs to increase the activity
        of adapting itself to this age.
To do this, it calls for help
    from the people living in the world
    who understand these times so well.

In this way, the Church is enriched
> by the development of human social life
> and all those who promote the values of the Gospels,
>> however that is done,
>> benefit the mission of the Church as well.

The Church has a visible social structure
> which is a sign of its unity in Christ.

Because of this social nature,
> we know that whoever contributes
> to the development of humankind on the level of
>> family,
>> culture,
>> economic and social life,
>> or national or international politics,
>>> when they order these
>>> according to the plan of God,
> also contributes to the life of the Church itself.

Even those who persecute the Church
> in some ways assist it.

45 In all this, the Church's assistance to the world
> and the world's assistance to the Church,
>> there is one single intention on our part:
>>> that God's reign be established
>>> and that all men and women
>>>> be made whole.

For the end of everything is life in God;
> for us this means life in Jesus.

Jesus is the answer to our longings,
> the center of the human race,
> the joy of every heart.

Enlivened and joined in Christ's Spirit,
> we recognize that, indeed,
> Jesus, the Christ, is the Alpha and the Omega,
> the beginning and the end of all that is.

Part 2:
Some Problems of Special Urgency
Preface

46 Having spoken in the council
> about the dignity of the human person
> and the work which all people are called to do

both as individuals and members of society,
we now turn our attention
to five specific questions:
marriage and the family;
human culture;
social, political, and economic life;
bonds among the nations;
war and peace.
We hope to speak of these under the light of Christ
so that Christians may be properly guided
and all humankind enlightened
as we search for answers
to complex questions.

Chapter I:
Fostering the Nobility of Marriage and the Family

47 Marriage and family life
are the bedrock of a healthy human society,
and we are pleased to see ways
in which these "partnerships of love"
are fostered today.
But there are also ways in which they are hindered,
such as polygamy,
divorce,
so-called free love,
excessive self-love,
the idealizing of pleasure,
and the illicit use of birth control.
It is also disrupted by
modern economic conditions,
social and psychological influences,
the demands of civil society,
and problems resulting from population growth.
In each of these cases,
anguish of conscience results for many
which is terribly painful and disruptive.
By reflecting on critical points,
(though not on all related matters)
we wish to support marriage and family life.

48 The partnership of married life and love, first of all,
is created by God and rooted in sexual union

when there is permanent,
     personal,
     and mutual consent.
Once agreed to, this bond is no longer purely human
     but now takes on a divine nature
     and is oriented toward having children
     and forming a family.
The two married partners
     render mutual service to each other
     through their sexual love and daily life
        leading them to total fidelity
        and unbreakable oneness.
Love of this sort wells up from the fountain of divine love
     which flows from Christ
        so that authentic married love
        comes from God.
It is for this reason that the Church
     treats marriage as a sacrament,
     a sign of God's faithful love of us,
     and a source of grace for the partners.
The love present in marriage is, then, really divine love
     expressed through sex and mutuality
     and lived out in the raising of the family.
Children, likewise, contribute in their own way
     to make their parents and the entire family holy.
Families thus share an interdependence
     providing support in hard times
     and sharing everyday life.

49 The love which a married couple shares
     is expressed and made perfect
     through sexual intercourse
        of which the Scriptures speak glowingly
        and which unites human and divine
           in mutual giving and bliss.
This is not mere eroticism, which ultimately fades,
     but an activity that involves the whole person
        in faithfulness and richness
        otherwise not known to humans.
Supported by mutual fidelity
     and made holy through the sacrament of matrimony,
     this love continues as the couple is faithful

in both mind and body,
in good times and in bad.
It therefore excludes either adultery or divorce.
Children should be taught about this
so, they, too, can enter marriages that are holy.

50 Marriage has several ends,
none of more or less account than the others.
Vital among them is the task of transmitting life
and educating those to whom it has been transmitted.
In this, parents cooperate in creation, a divine activity,
and must enter into this thoughtfully.
They should take into account those already born
and those foreseen,
considering both the material and spiritual conditions
of the times and of their family's state.
They then consult the interests of the family group,
of temporal society, and of the Church's teachings.
The parents should, then, ultimately make this judgment
in the sight of God,
following their conscience,
enlightened by divine law,
and guided by the Church.
Thus, parents sometimes stop having children
and yet maintain their love,
for the purpose of marriage is not solely tied
to procreation.
The mutual love of the spouses, too,
must be embodied in a right manner;
it must grow and ripen.

51 This can be very difficult if sexual loving is ended
in order to prevent conception
and can endanger the bond
as well as the quality of family life.
We reject wholeheartedly a solution to this
which involves the taking of life
through abortion or the killing of infants.
Since the transmission of human life
is not merely a human activity,
sexual intercourse and responsible conception
must be harmonized.

Decisions made toward this end
  should be based on objective standards
    which reflect divine love.
Catholics are not allowed to use methods of birth regulation
  which are disapproved of
  by the teaching authority of the Church.
How all of this will be understood in our day and age
  has been handed over to a special commission
  which will report soon to the pope
    and, for that reason,
    this is all we will say here about it.

52 The family is a school of more profound humanity
  and needs the communion of minds
  and joint decisions of spouses
  as well as the cooperation of the children
    to be maintained.
Having the father present is essential,
  and allowing the mother her domestic role
  is also needed, though this should not undermine
    the legitimate social progress of women.
Children should be prepared for independence
  and not forced into marriage.
Hence families are the foundation of society,
  and governments should support them.
Those skilled in science, too,
  can support the regulation of births
  and peace of conscience,
    especially those in medicine,
    biology,
    social science,
    and psychology.
Organizations outside the family can also offer support
  especially for children and spouses.
And, finally, spouses themselves,
  joined in authentic sexual love,
  share harmony of mind and mutual holiness;
    they are a witness to the presence of God
    and the mystery of love.

220 The Story and Promise of Vatican II

Chapter II:
The Proper Development of Culture

53 The cultivation of the goods and values of nature
        are the basis of the authentic human person.
        People live in both culture and nature.
There are, of course, a plurality of cultures
        each having a historical aspect,
                as well as a social dimension,
                a sociological sense,
                and a unique ethnic character.
All culture implies "community living"
        and includes patterns for sharing wealth,
        various ways of laboring;
            of language;
            of religious practice;
            of forming customs;
            of making laws and courts;
            of advancing the arts, sciences, and beauty.

54 Because of all the changes that have taken place recently
        in social and cultural life,
           we can actually call this a "new age"
        in human history.
The enormous growth of natural, human, and social science,
        not to mention communications and technology,
           has paved the way
           for a modern refinement of culture.
Critical judgment has been shaped to a fine edge
        by the exact sciences, for example.
Human behavior is explained more fully
        by psychological research.
Historical studies throw new light on our past,
        helping us see how changeable
           and evolutionary the world is.
All over the world, customs are more uniform,
        lifestyles are similarly urban,
        and new ways of thinking and using leisure
        are everywhere.
Thus, little by little, a more universal form
        of human culture is developing
        through which the unity of humankind
        is being fostered.

55 We are increasingly aware
    that we are the authors of this new culture,
    that we are directly responsible for it
      and will live under it.
There is a new humanism in the world today
    which defines us first and foremost
    as responsible for each other.

56 All of this raises some difficult new questions
    for us today.
How can we continue to increase exchange among cultures
    while at the same time
    maintain the identity of the small community,
      preserve ancestral wisdom,
      and save the uniqueness of each people?
How can the vitality and growth of a new culture
    harmonize with the heritage of tradition?
How can branches of knowledge shoot out quickly
    while at the same time we undertake
    a necessary synthesis of them
      so men and women can still grow in wisdom
      through contemplation and wonder?
How can all women and men on earth share somehow
    in the new technology?
And finally, how will we maintain the independence
    which culture claims for itself
    without developing a humanism devoid of God?

57 Here are some principles which we can follow
    to begin to offer answers to these questions.
First of all, faith and culture work together
    with many of the same aims and goals.
The fact that faith points people toward divine life
    does not diminish people's attention to human life
      because the two are intimately linked.
Most aspects of culture elevate the human family
    to a more sublime understanding
    of truth, goodness, beauty, and fairness.
Even though there is a temptation in science
    and under modern scientific thinking
    to doubt everything not observable,
      nonetheless, it also prepares us

to remain close to God.
Furthermore, modern advancements
provide many positive values,
including the study of science,
fidelity to truth in this study,
teamwork in technology,
international solidarity,
the role of experts in helping all,
and an eagerness to improve
the human standard of living.

58 Second, the Church is not bound
to any particular culture or period of history,
and human and religious culture advance
as one reality.
The Good News of Christ
mixes with life and human culture
to combat and remove error and evil,
to purify and elevate the morality of peoples,
and to assist spiritual qualities to blossom.

59 Third, the purpose of culture is the benefit of humans,
the good of the community and of society.
It is the role of culture to develop
the human spirit of wonder;
understanding;
contemplation;
the formation of personal judgments;
and the development of a religious,
moral,
and social sense of self.
Toward this end, the rights of the individual
and the needs of the community
are both safeguarded
within the limits of the common good.
Cultural development requires that freedom be in place,
freedom to search for truth,
voice one's mind,
and publicize one's beliefs.
Public authority should make this possible everywhere.
60 Because it is possible today
to liberate most people from ignorance,

Christians have the urgent duty to provide education
wherever it is needed.
This will make it possible for a fuller participation
in cultural life for many people
who otherwise would not be included,
especially country people and laborers,
as well as women.
Regarding women especially,
everyone is responsible for ensuring
that their specific role in cultural life is fostered.
61 With so much new knowledge today,
almost no one can grasp it all
and unify all aspects of human understanding
in his or her thinking.
Nonetheless, it is essential that we maintain a view
of humans as whole persons,
including intellect, will, and conscience.
Taking advantage of increased leisure for reading,
sports, and physical activities,
time with family, and travel
will enrich people and help them reach
an emotional balance.

62 It has proven difficult sometimes
to harmonize culture with the Church
but it is necessary to do that.
Recent studies and findings of science,
history,
and philosophy
raise new questions about life
and demand new theological investigations.
Furthermore, theologians are invited
to find more suitable ways
to communicate doctrine to the people
of their times.
The deposit of faith or revealed truths are one thing,
but the manner in which it is expressed
is another.
Pastors can employ psychology and sociology
to bring faith more effectively to life.
Literature and the arts can elevate men and women
to new planes of understanding

about our place in history
and the meaning of these times.
The Church should give recognition, therefore,
to these arts, including new forms of them,
and introduce them into the sanctuary
when appropriate.
Christ's faithful can thereby live in closer union
with their neighbors
if religious practice and morality keep pace
with science and its theories.
Theological inquiry should seek a profound understanding
of revealed truth
without neglecting close contact with its own times.
Lay people ought to be trained in the sacred sciences
and some will deepen these studies
by their own labors.
And finally, everyone possesses
lawful freedom of inquiry and thought
and the freedom to express their minds humbly
but with courage about those matters
in which they enjoy competence.

Chapter III:
Socio-Economic Life

63 Once again in the arena of economics,
we declare that the dignity and wholeness
of the human person
must be honored as the center of focus.
As we have noted in other areas of human activity,
the economic life of women and men
is characterized
by an increasing domination of nature,
closer and more intense ties among citizens,
more mutual interdependence among nations,
and frequent government intervention.
At the same time, there has been great economic progress
which has made it possible to provide
for the increasing needs of the human race.
Still, there are reasons for anxiety today.
Many people are so captivated by their economic lives
that they seem nearly hypnotized by it,
both in wealthy nations as well as poorer ones.

We have the ability to make everyone on Earth
    economically comfortable,
      yet so often a minority is served and a majority suffer.
Hence, luxury and misery rub shoulders,
    and while the wealthy are able to choose
    among competing economic goods,
      the deprived have almost no such choices
      and live in subhuman conditions.
There often seems to be a lack of balance even with a nation
    among various industries:
      farming,
      manufacturing,
      and service industries.
And the imbalance among nations
    threatens the peace of the world!
Because all of this is true,
    this council now turns its attention
    to this important and dynamic human activity
    to reinforce certain principles
      and set forth specific guidelines
      to assist in economic development.

64 First and foremost,
    technical progress must be fostered
    to make it more possible to provide for all.
Along with this, a spirit of initiative,
    an eagerness to create and expand enterprises,
    the adaptation of methods of production,
    and the hard work of all who engage in production,
      all of these must be fostered too.
But here is the principle:
    the purpose of this is not to make anyone rich;
    it is not to give some the means of dominating others.
The purpose of this is to be in the service of all humans
    in terms of their intellectual,
      moral,
      and religious lives.
Economic development must, therefore,
    be carried out according to clear moral standards
    so that God's desire for humans is realized.

65 Not only that but secondly,

economic development must be under the control
of the human family, working together,
        not left to the sole judgment of a few
        who possess economic or political power.
Within a nation, the citizens must decide these matters
        together among themselves.
Among nations, all affected parties should participate.
In all cases, people and their rights come first
        and production is the secondary aim.
Citizens have the right and duty to contribute
        according to their skills
        to economic development and production.
Those with the means to do so
        should not let their investment funds lay fallow
        but should put them to use to employ others!

66 Third, and very importantly,
        vigorous efforts must be made as quickly as possible
        to reduce or remove
                the immense economic inequalities
                which now exist.
The demands of justice require this.
In particular, farmers and country people
        must be helped to receive their just compensation.
Immigrant or migrant workers should be welcomed
        and discrimination against them avoided,
        and they should not be treated as mere tools
                of production.
And in all places,
        leaders should take care to provide suitable work
        for all who are capable of it.
In situations where industry is changing quickly,
        as in the use of automation, for example,
        care should be taken that workers still have labor.
And those who are unable to work,
        who are old or infirm,
        should also be cared for.

67 Fourth, it is our clear principle
        that human labor as a part of production
        is superior to other elements of economic life.
It is ordinarily by his or her labors

that a woman or man supports her or himself.
It is also how humans serve one another,
    join together in common efforts of charity,
    and become partners in God's unfolding creation.
Jesus himself was such a worker.
Hence, everyone has an actual duty to work,
    and society has a duty to make work available
    and to be sure that wages are fair.
Toward this end and in keeping with principles of justice,
    working conditions must be suitable and safe,
    and economic slavery must be ended.
In fact, work-life should be adapted
    to the needs of the persons doing it,
    especially mothers and the aged.
Finally, workers should be able to develop as persons
    through their labors
    and to have ample leisure time
        for family, cultural life, and prayer.

68 Fifth, workers themselves should share
    in the decision making which affects their workplace
        as well as their industry.
Freely founded labor unions are a human right
    and provide an orderly way
    for workers to participate
    as long as their means are peaceful
        and conflict is resolved through negotiation
        and without resort to violence.
Workers have the right to elect their own representatives
    to these unions
    and be part of them without reprisal.

69 Sixth, the Earth and all it contains
    are meant for all to share fairly.
Whatever forms of ownership are followed,
    attention must always be paid
    to this universal purpose,
    and all the goods of the earth
        should benefit all the people of the earth.
Hence, we are bound to come to the relief of the poor
    and to do so not only out of our leftovers
        but out of our very subsistence.

Today the poor number among the majority
     so that we call on all people and nations
     with the means to do so
     to undertake a genuine sharing of their goods.
In less advanced societies,
     customs which no longer work
     should be updated so all are cared for.
Social services which support the family
     should be encouraged everywhere
     but not so much that the citizens
          form negative attitudes toward society.

70 Seventh, toward this end,
     the distribution of goods and services
     around the world should not be limited to charity
          but should be directed toward helping
          people find employment and sufficient income.
This will require economic planning
     so that today's needs are not met
     at the expense of tomorrow's.
Furthermore, underdeveloped nations
     should receive special attention
     in economic planning.
Special care should be taken that such nations
     not suffer when money values decline.

71 Eighth, it is essential for people to own the resources
     of their nations
     and to have some control over material goods.
Such private ownership or another form of private dominion
     over material goods
     provides necessary independence.
It adds incentives for carrying on one's work
     and constitutes a prerequisite for civil liberties.
This is not to be seen to be in conflict
     with necessary public ownership
     of specific resources that serve the public good.
In situations where the majority own most of the land
     while the minority have none or very little,
     steps should be taken toward balance.
Often in these situations, the workers
     are paid too little to live on

and lack decent housing
    while the owners and merchants
    take all the profits.
Some people live in virtual slavery as a result of this,
    and all gains in culture and dignity are impossible.
Reforms are to be instituted in these cases
    and may include the re-division of land,
    cooperative enterprises,
    or educational assistance to people
        to help make them more productive.

72 In closing this discussion of economic life,
    let us say that Christians who work for justice
    and take an active role in economic development
    are making a significant contribution
        to the peace of the world
        and the prosperity of humankind.
They help permeate the world
    with the spirit of the beatitudes
    and grow in love as they work for justice.

Chapter IV:
The Life of the Political Community
73 Changes are taking place today
    in how people are governed,
    and these include a growing awareness
        of the rights of minorities
        and of people's desire for freedom—
    freedom of assembly,
        of common action,
        and of religion.
There seems to be a broader spirit of cooperation
    taking hold around the world
    based on people's inner sense of justice,
        goodness,
        and the common good.
The best way to achieve a political life which serves people
    is to foster an inner sense of justice,
        generosity, and service of others.
We also want to strengthen fundamental beliefs
    about the nature of politics
    and about the proper limits of governments.

74 Acting alone, individuals or families
    are not sufficiently able to establish
    all that is needed for fully human life.
Hence, we group together to provide for those conditions
    in which people can become their fully human,
        created, and graced selves.
Authority in this collective enterprise
    is a good thing and very much needed
    to prevent people from fighting
        as they pursue their own needs.
Such authority should function more as a moral force
    than as a tyrant.
Hence, the political community exists for the sake
    of the common good, not for its own sake,
    and when it is legally established in a nation,
        citizens are bound to obey it.
If such political authority exceeds it bounds
    and violates the rights or dignity of anyone,
    then citizens are bound to defend themselves
        against such abuses.
Whatever form of government is chosen in a nation
    it should make people more civilized,
        peace-loving,
        and full of desire for the common good.
75 Political systems should act without discrimination
    and allow all citizens the chance
    to participate freely and actively in forming a state
        and choosing leaders.
Citizens, therefore, have a duty to vote,
    and leaders are to be praised for stepping forth.
A system of law is also a good thing
    when it protects rights
    and furnishes the state with order and support.
But we should be on guard against granting government
    too much authority or seeking too much from it
    because that weakens the sense of responsibility
        on the part of individuals,
            families,
            and groups.
If individual rights are temporarily suspended
    during an emergency,

they should be restored very quickly.
Citizens, for their part, should be loyal to their country
      but not blind to the needs of the rest of the world.
They should be aware that there will be differences
      about how to best govern
      and enter into the public debate with a good heart.
Those who are suited for it
      should enter the art of politics
      without thought of personal gain
         or the benefit of bribery.
Such leaders should oppose
      injustice and oppression,
      oligarchy or arbitrary use of power,
      and intolerance for diversity.

76 We must never confuse the Church
      with the political community
      nor bind it to any political system.
In fact, the political community and the Church
      are mutually independent and self-governing.
The Church's contribution is to introduce love and justice
      into society, not to govern it.
But it is also the Church's legitimate work
      to preach the faith in freedom,
      to teach her social doctrines,
      and to discharge her duty among people
         without hindrance.
The Church also has the right to pass moral judgments
      when the salvation of souls is at stake
      for it is the Church's task to reveal,
         cherish, and ennoble
      all that is true, good, and beautiful
         in the human community.

Chapter V:
The Fostering of Peace
and the Promotion of a Community of Nations

77 "Those who work for peace
      shall be called children of God"
      according to the Gospel of Matthew,
      and, indeed, in our day, these words
         shed new light on the human family's

growth toward full development.
For we live in a time of war and the threat of war,
        and we are in a tremendous human crisis.
We wish to cooperate with all people of goodwill
        to help establish a stable, lasting peace on Earth.
78 Peace, we believe, is not merely the absence of war.
        Nor is it reduced to a silent, cold
                standoff where the parties remain armed.
        And it is not an outcome of dictatorship.
What is it, then?
        Indeed, what is "peace"?
Peace is a harmony built into human society
        by God, the divine Founder of all life,
        and it is a direct outcome of justice.
Such a peace is not attained once and for all
        but is continuously built up
        as people control their passions
                and governments remain vigilant.
But even this is not enough.
        For peace is the fruit of love as well.
It cannot be obtained and safeguarded
        unless men and women freely and trustingly
        share with one another their inner spirits and talents.
It is based on a firm determination to respect others,
        and to live actual lives of sister and brotherhood.
Without such love, peace absolutely cannot prevail
        in our time.
For all of this flows from the peace of Christ
        who first loved us
        and dedicated himself to us.
We urge all Christians, therefore,
        to join with all peacemakers in the world
        to plead for peace and bring it about.
We praise those who renounce violence
        and find other ways to settle disputes
        where fairness for all is assured.
We dream of the day when we will say with Isaiah,
        "They shall beat their swords into plowshares
                and their spears into pruning hooks;
                one nation shall not raise the sword
                against another,
                nor shall they train for war again."

79 Despite this great dream of all people,
        savage warfare goes on all over the world,
        in fact, more savage than ever before.
Having considered all this,
        we in this council remind everyone
        first and foremost about the permanent, binding force
                of natural law,
                which is the law written in our very hearts.
Any action which deliberately conflicts with this law
        or any command ordering someone else to do so
                is criminal.
Blind obedience will excuse no one from this.

Among the actions which fall into this category,
        that is, which conflict with natural law,
        is any methodical extermination of an entire people,
                nation,
                or ethnic minority.
No case can be made for such an action!
        It is always horrendously wrong!
Those who oppose such actions
        are highly praised.
International agreements to make military activity
        less inhumane
        should be strengthened and obeyed.

Now, on the subject of war,
        it clearly still exists on Earth
        and, therefore, governments cannot be denied
        the right to legitimate defense when attacked;
                indeed, governments have a duty
                to protect their citizens.
But it is one thing to defend oneself or one's nation
        and another to offensively move against others.
All who volunteer for armed-service duty
        should think of themselves as agents of peace,
                security,
                and freedom.

80 We undertake an evaluation of war today
        with a new attitude

because of the presence of weapons
of total destruction.
Therefore, we hereby utterly condemn total war,
and following the teachings of Pope John XXIII
in *Pacem in Terris*
and Pope Paul VI at the United Nations,
we issue this declaration:
Any act of war aimed indiscriminately at the destruction
of entire cities or of extensive areas
along with their populations
is a crime against God and humanity itself
and merits absolute
and unhesitating condemnation!
What is so unique about this situation
is that world events might unfold on their own
in such a way that someone may decide
to use such a weapon.
In order to help prevent this from happening,
we bishops of the entire world
urge all world leaders to consider
the awesome responsibility which is theirs
when their nations possess such weapons.
81 We also realize that such weapons,
based on modern science
and capable of total destruction,
are amassed with the thought in mind
that having them will deter an enemy
from attacking in the first place.
Many regard this as an effective way to keep the peace.
We believe, on the contrary,
that this is not a safe way to keep peace at all.
The so-called "balance" which results
is unsure and unsteady
and the threat of war only increases
as the number of weapons does.
Furthermore, while vast fortunes are spent
to purchase and build these weapons,
the poor continue to starve,
disagreements among nations are not healed,
and the world lives in terrible anxiety.
We repeat it: the arms race is a treacherous trap
for all of humanity

and one which injures the poor
to an intolerable degree.
Let us work together to seek another approach,
one more worthy of the dignity of humanity.
If we fail to do this, we do not know where the evil path
on which we tread will lead.

82 Peace, then, must be born of mutual trust between nations
rather than a doubtful outcome of their fear
of one another's weapons.
We commit ourselves to work for the day
when war—all war—can be completely outlawed
by international consent.
In the meantime, let us move toward disarmament,
not unilaterally but in every nation.
Many world leaders are now working to end war,
and we commend you!
It is time to put aside purely national interests
so that the whole community of humankind
can find peace together.

The basis for this is in each person's change of heart
as we regard the entire world
and those tasks which we can perform in unison
for the betterment of all people.
Peace will not come until hatreds end;
until contempt for others ends;
until distrust, unbending ideologies,
and divisions cease.
The Church now takes its stand in the midst
of these anxieties
which are felt in every nation of the world.
We intend to continually say to all:
Now is the proper time for change!

83 If peace is indeed to succeed,
the causes of discord must be reduced,
especially injustice
which results from economic inequalities,
from a quest for power,
or from contempt for personal rights.

84 The way to do this is for the human family
        sharing this planet together
        to create for itself a system of governance
                which is sufficient to meet the demands
                of these modern times.
We have the beginnings in current international agencies,
        and cooperation among all people,
                regardless of their religion,
                is central to this.
The Church is delighted with the growing
        cooperative spirit among nations
        both Christian and non-Christians.

85 These international efforts should also be extended
        to the economic field
        where wealthy and developed nations
        assist others in procuring
        the necessary material goods
                for a more vibrant quality of life.
If this is to work, we will have to reduce
        excessive desire for profit,
        nationalistic pretensions,
        the lust for political domination,
        militaristic thinking,
        and schemes designed to promote ideologies.

86 Toward this end, we can offer some guidelines:
First, as nations develop
        they should firmly hold
        the complete human fulfillment of their citizens
                as the goal of their efforts.
Second, advanced nations have a duty
        to assist developing people toward this end.
Third, the entire world should organize together
        to provide for economic growth
        but should do so taking into account
                the rights of all to determine their own fate
                and the duty of all to assist one another.
Fourth, there is a pressing need to reform
        the very structures of economic activity,
        but nations should be wary of solutions
                which nibble away at human spirituality

or wholeness.

87 We do recognize the need in some places
      to regulate and reduce population growth.
Every effort should be made to distribute food and goods
      more fairly to all
      and, indeed, to increase production when possible.
And since so many people are concerned today
      about controlling population growth,
      we urge that whatever steps are taken
         be in accord with the moral law.
The question of how many children a couple should have
      is a matter of conscience
      and not of government-imposed rules.
This parental decision takes into account
      educational and social conditions
      and these modern times.
People should be made aware in a wise manner
      of scientific advances which can help them
      arrange the number of their children.
The reliability of such methods should be proven,
      and they should be in harmony with our ethics.

88 Given all we have said,
      let us add that Christians also have a duty
      to support personally those who are poor.
Certain wealthy nations, with mainly Christian populations,
      must see the deprivation of the others,
         the torment,
         disease,
         and hunger in the rest of the world.
Well-organized efforts to share resources
      should be undertaken,
      ecumenically when possible,
         to alleviate suffering everywhere.
As was true in the early years of the Church,
      Christians should meet the needs of these poor
      out of their own subsistence
         and not only from what is "left over."
Collections among Christians should be taken
      throughout the entire world
      in cooperation, when possible, with other Christians.

89 The Church stands among the nations
        as a catalyst for this activity.
To achieve this, the Church must be present
        among the nations in a thoroughgoing way,
            both through her members
            as well as institutionally.

90 Toward this end, we at this council
        now recommend the establishment of an agency
            of the universal Church.
This agency will have the task of promoting justice,
        stimulating the Catholic community to participate
        and work for social justice   on an international level.
It will take its place among other agencies
        and help end the terrible hardships
        felt by people around the world today.

Conclusion

91 These proposals, dealing with many modern challenges,
        are meant for all people,
        whether or not they believe in God.
What we have said here is very general
        but it is rooted in the gospel
        and we hope further development
            of these ideas
            will produce action.

92 Indeed, the Church itself is a sign of cooperation
        based on honest dialogue.
This requires that we ourselves foster within the Church
        mutual esteem,
        reverence,
        harmony,
        and the full recognition of legitimate diversity.
"For the bonds which unite the faithful are mightier
        than anything dividing them.
Hence, let there be unity in what is necessary;
        freedom in what is unsettled,
        and charity in any case."
We embrace those not yet in full communion with us
        to whom we are linked by faith

and a common bond of charity.
Likewise, we embrace those who do not believe in Christ
    who also await unity and peace.

We fervently wish to have a frank conversation
    with all people of goodwill,
        everyone who seeks goodness and truth,
            excluding no one,
            even those who hate the Church,
                so we can build peace with all.

93 There is nothing, in short,
    for which Christians yearn more
    than to serve the people of the modern world
        generously and effectively.
We Christians shoulder a gigantic task
    which is to introduce love into the world,
    that love which we receive ourselves from Christ.
May Christ be with us in our work!

Learn more online

- Comprehensive summaries of the remaining twelve council documents.
- Additional tools for understanding the council.
- Pastoral resources for putting the council into practice today.

**Visit
http://Vatican2.center**

Bill Huebsch

Bill Huebsch lives in St. Paul, Minnesota, USA and Milverton, Somerset, England. He teaches on the adjunct faculty of the Institute for Pastoral Studies, Loyola University Chicago. Bill is an award-winning author, a gardener, a husband, a university professor, and an advocate for the poor. He maintains a busy international lecture schedule.

Endnotes

1   Since the close of Vatican II, Pope John XXIII has been canonized so that his correct title today is St. John XXIII. His original name was Angelo Giuseppe Roncalli. He was born on November 25, 1881, in Sotto il Monte, Italy. He died June 3, 1963, in Rome and was beatified on September 3, 2000. He was canonized on April 27, 2014. His feast day is October 11. For purposes of this text, however, we will use the name current with the Second Vatican Council: Pope John XXIII or simply Pope John.

2   McDonough, William. From an article entitled, "Raymond A. Lucker (1927-2001): Bishop-herald of catechesis for conversion in an adult church," (2007).

3   Austin Flannery, OP, *Vatican Council II*. Available as a revised translation in inclusive language. (Dublin: Dominican, 1996). Also see Walter M. Abbott SJ, *The Documents of Vatican II*. Guild Press/ America Pr./ Association Pr.; 1 edition (1966).

4   The Latin version of the texts of the Council are readily available at the Vatican website. They're also available there in a dozen other languages of the world.

5   Council Daybooks of Vatican II. Washington DC: National Catholic Welfare Conference (1966). 1189 pages in three volumes.

6   Outstanding in this genre are a number of important works. One is the journal kept by Yves Congar OP, *My Journal of the Council*. Mary John Ronayne OP (Translator), Mary Cecily Boulding OP (Translator). Michael Glazier; Translated edition (June 1, 2012). This project is more than 1100 pages long but filled with important details and insights about the council. Also important for understanding how this council fit into the history of the ecumenical councils of the church is Norman Tanner's definitive translation of the major documents of the councils: *Decrees of the Ecumenical Councils* (2 vols). (Washington DC: Georgetown Univ Press, 1990). The most authoritative commentary on the docu-

ments themselves is probably still Herbert Vorgrimler's *Commentary on the Documents of Vatican II* (5 vols). (New York: Herder and Herder, 1967-1969). Another source is a series of articles in *Vatican II: An Interfaith Appraisal*, edited by John Miller and published by University of Notre Dame Press in 1966. There are many other such sources available.

7   Giuseppe Alberigo and Joseph Komonchak, *History of Vatican II*, Vols 1, 2 & 3. The first major and exhaustive history of the council. This work is essential to anyone who wants to fully understand the provenance of the various documents and conciliar activities. Edited by Giuseppe Alberigo and Joseph Komonchak. (Maryknoll, NY: Orbis and Leuven: Peeters, 1995 and 1996 respectively)

8   Xavier Rynne, *Vatican Council II*. Orbis Books (August 1, 1999). 610 pages. Rynne used a pen name to publish articles in *The New Yorker* magazine during the council. He was a Redemptorist priest, Francis Xavier Murphy CSsR. Rynne was his mother's maiden name. His inside account of the council was frank, colorful, and sometimes irreverent.

9   Robert B Kaiser, *Pope, Council, and World: The Story of Vatican II*. Andesite Press (August 8, 2015). 292 pages.

10   John O'Malley, *What Happened at Vatican II?* Belknap Press of Harvard University Press; 1st Edition (September 30, 2008). 400 pages.

11   Richard Gaillardetz and Catherine Clifford, *Keys to the Council: Unlocking the Teaching of Vatican II*. Liturgical Press (February 1, 2012). 224 pages.

12   "The Canonical Doctrine of Reception" by James A. Coriden (no date given). Coriden is the Academic Dean Emeritus at Washington Theological Union, where he also teaches canon law. Ordained in 1957, he holds degrees in theology, canon law, and civil law. He has written most often on matters of church discipline and ministry, and has served as co-editor of the Canon Law Society of America's commentary on the Revised Code of Canon Law.

13 Pope John XXIII, *Journal of a Soul*. (Trans by Dorothy White. New York: McGraw Hill, 1965).

14 By Professor Ted Ross SJ in his "History of Vatican II" course in 1980.

15 Quoted in John O'Malley, *What Happened* (cited above), page 19.

16 Pope Paul VI was canonized after the end of the Second Vatican Council so his title now is St. Paul VI. His original name was Giovanni Battista Montini. He was born on September 26, 1897 at Concesio (near Brescia) Italy. He died on August 6, 1978. He was beatified on October 19, 2014 and canonized on October 14, 2018. His feast day is September 26. For purposes of this text, however, we will use the name current with the Second Vatican Council: Pope Paul VI or simply Pope Paul.

17 By Professor Ted Ross SJ.

18 Xavier Rynne tells colorful stories about these coffee bars and other elements of the council in his work, cited above.

19 See for example *Mirari Vos* from Gregory XVI in 1832, the *Syllabus of Errors* from Pius IX in 1864, *Providentissimus Deus* from Leo XIII in 1893, *Lamentabili* and *Pascendi* from Pius X in 1907, *Mortalium Animos* in 1928, and *Casti Connubi* in 1930 both from Pius XI, and *Humani Generis* from Pius XII in 1950 upon which followed a purge of all those who were considered guilty of modern forms of thought.

20 Komonchak, Joseph. "Pope John XXIII and the Idea of an Ecumenical Council," 2011.

21 Sonya A. Quitslund, *Beauduin, A Prophet Vindicated* (New York: Newman Press, 1973).

22 See *My Journal of the Council*, cited above. Page 282.

23 According to Professor Ted Ross SJ.

24 Much of the inside information about the death of Pope John comes from an extensive interview with his long-time secretary and friend, Monsignor Loris Capovilla. To honor his service to

Pope John, Capovilla was made a cardinal in 2014, the oldest in the world at that time. The interview with Monsignor Capovilla was conducted in the mid-1990s in preparation for the filming of *The Faithful Revolution: Vatican II*, (RCL-Benziger, 1997).

25 This material first appeared in Bill Huebsch. *The Spiritual Wisdom of St. John XXIII* (Twenty-Third Pubs, 2014).

26 John O'Malley treats this change (and the long debate on the constitution on the church) very well in his *What Happened at Vatican II*, work cited above, chapter five.

27 "The Catholic Church and Contraception." *The New Yorker*. This piece is found in Xavier Rynne's work cited above.

28 Joseph Ratzinger, *Theological Highlights of Vatican II*, (Paulist Press; 1996). A revised edition was published in 2009. Pages 114-116.

29 Balducci, Ernesto. *John "The Transitional Pope."* Trans. Dorothy White. (New York: McGraw-Hill, 1965), p. 31.

30 This summary was first published in 1996 in Bill Huebsch, *Vatican II in Plain English* (Dallas: Thomas More Press) but some of the insights reported in this revision come from *The Council and the Future*, Mario von Galli, 1966, McGraw-Hill, New York.

Made in the USA
Middletown, DE
24 November 2021

52503989R00146